COPING WITH BLINDNESS

COPING
WITH
BLINDNESS
Personal Tales of Blindness Rehabilitation

ALVIN ROBERTS

Southern Illinois University Press
Carbondale and Edwardsville

Library of Congress Cataloging-in-Publication Data
Roberts, Alvin.
Coping with blindness : personal tales of blindness
rehabilitation / Alvin Roberts.
    p. cm.
    1. Blind—Rehabilitation—United States.   I. Title.
HV1795.R63   1998
362.4'1'092273—dc21   98-6840
[b]   CIP
ISBN 0-8093-2160-2 (alk. paper)

The paper used in this publication meets the minimum
requirements of American National Standard for Information
Sciences—Permanence of Paper for Printed Library Materials,
ANSI Z39.48-1984. ○

To the few hundred committed teachers and counselors,
blind and sighted, who fan out across the nation every
morning, providing rehabilitation services to the sixty
thousand American citizens who become blind every year

CONTENTS

Contents

PREFACE

After forty years of enabling blind people to cope with the challenges of living in a world of seeing people and striving to remove societal barriers so that the blind could fully participate, I could not write a book that did not convey a social message or intent. My intent (or, at least, my hope) is that through these stories, some of the 1.7 million Americans who are blind or are in the process of losing their vision will be reassured that blindness need not be the end of active life but rather the beginning of a life in which they will depend on their residual senses. I hope that this reassurance will be conveyed by the effectiveness with which the teachers and counselors portrayed in these narratives assist visually impaired persons to reenter the mainstream of society.

Beyond my desire to assure those experiencing visual loss that competent professional help with the adjustment process is available, I also wish to acquaint readers with the humorous aspect of the daily work of this small, dedicated group of professionals. Those who become blind bring to this unchosen condition the full array of personality characteristics, including a sense of humor. In fact, some of the funniest people I have known were blind. Take Bob Ingersol, a blind man from my hometown, for instance. Many people who knew and loved him were often the recipients of Bob's practical jokes. As a high school student, far from home at the Illinois School for the

Blind in Jacksonville, I looked forward to Bob's encouraging and news-filled letters, which usually ended with such bits of earthy humor as, "Some final advice from your friendly stock broker: Sit on your American Can and hold your Water." Lloyd, a blind piano tuner, would slip a few pieces of the family silver in the coat pockets of friends who were visiting for the first time in order to enjoy their reactions when he "accidentally" discovered these items while helping them on with their wraps. Then there was Floyd, a lifelong friend, who would respond to the inquiries of waitresses as to how much cream he liked in his coffee with "just enough to see if there is a fly floating in it." Of course, these people were serious, hard-working folks most of the time, but, like their seeing peers, they had their lighter side. I have observed that an active sense of humor is a definite asset to those who are required to adjust to a life without vision, and it certainly makes the work of the adjustment teacher or counselor less stressful and more enjoyable. If these accounts can help to dispel a commonly held notion that blind people are uniformly somber and that those who assist them work under grim conditions, this book may succeed in lowering society's generalized fear of blindness.

The motivation to write something that could provide emotional reassurance to the public, particularly the elderly who are most at risk of becoming visually impaired, has been with me for many years. The problem was "packaging the message," as the advertising and public relations people put it. My office and home library are filled with books on how to live with blindness, including one I wrote, *Psychosocial Rehabilitation of the Blind*, but, according to various public opinion surveys, society's fear of blindness has not been reduced by this wealth of published material. In order to succeed in replacing fear, which creates myths and apprehension, with facts and common sense, I believed it would be necessary to communicate factual material about blindness by anchoring it to positive emotions and optimism—a formidable task.

We have known since antiquity that facts are remembered longer when presented in stories of people and events. This is why most of us learn history better from historical fiction than from history texts. At some point, it occurred to me that the most effective avenue to the emotional acceptance of facts about blindness adjustment would be to let the public read about real, believable people engaged with their teachers and counselors in the process of learning to live with visual impairment. Personal experience and conversations with colleagues provided me with a wealth of incidents on which to base stories of workers with the blind going about their daily tasks. My task was to develop these incidents into believable stories, adding descriptive material, action, and conversation to enhance plausibility and create interest, amusement, or excitement. Although some characters have been invented to round out the stories, several colleagues who furnished material for a particular narrative—such as Louis Davis, Dorothy Dykema, Harker Miley, Edith Ingersol, and Verle Wessel— are named. And all of the accounts are factual and accurate regarding counseling or instruction and blindness adjustment techniques, strategies, and methods.

PART ONE

LEARNING TO LIVE WITH BLINDNESS: REHABILITATION TEACHING

I f you suddenly became blind, from whom would you immediately seek services? A physiotherapist? An occupational therapist? A vocational counselor? A psychologist? You might need the services of any or all of these professionals at some time during your adjustment to visual impairment, but your most immediate need would be the ability to carry out the necessary tasks of day-to-day living. You would need some techniques that do not require sight for performing such routine tasks as color-matching your clothes, identifying your medication, pouring your morning coffee, and setting the thermostat on your heating or cooling system. In other words, you would need a rehabilitation teacher.

Don't be discouraged by such a clinical-sounding name. Although rehabilitation teachers are highly trained professionals who enable visually impaired persons to carry out virtually all of their daily activities, they do not practice their profession within the limited confines of some distant hospital or rehabilitation center. In fact, many states have a commission, bureau, or department for the visually impaired that employs rehabilitation teachers to instruct blind persons in their own homes using their own appliances. To emphasize this fact, these teachers were originally known as "home teachers of the adult blind."

Rehabilitation teaching had its beginning with the London Home Teaching Society in 1855. Teachers were dispatched throughout England to teach embossed reading systems to the blind. "Home teaching" came to America with the establishment of the Pennsylvania Home Teaching Society in 1882. Today, rehabilitation teaching programs exist in every state. In addition to the delivery of instruction directly into the homes of visually impaired persons, many public and private rehabilitation hospitals and centers now employ rehabilitation teachers as members of multidisciplinary teams, which can also include mobility instructors, vocational counselors, social workers, and psychologists.

Besides instructing visually impaired people in such daily living tasks as reading in Braille, writing with tactile hand guides, and homemaking, rehabilitation teachers are also prepared to understand the emotional impact of visual loss on the impaired person and his or her family. Teachers use this understanding to enhance the success of the teaching program. For example, one of the first assurances a visually impaired person might receive from a rehabilitation teacher is the information that he or she is not the only person facing the loss of sight on that particular day. The knowledge that 179 other people in the nation have also experienced visual loss during the previous twenty-four hours may lessen the feeling of isolation. Applying the formula of .00253 legally blind persons per 1,000 people in the United States, the Illinois Department of Rehabilitation Services estimates that there are 29,182 legally blind people in the state, for example. (Legal blindness is defined as visual acuity of 20/200 in the better eye or a visual field of 20 degrees or less [180 degrees is considered normal].) Application of the .00253 formula to an estimated United States population of 260 million results in a projection of 657,800 legally blind people in the nation. Of this number, we estimate that 65,780 became blind within the past year—approximately 180 within the past twenty-four hours, as mentioned above.

Another service provided by the rehabilitation teacher is the organization of support groups composed of just such newly blinded persons. In these groups, people receive encouragement from each other and knowledge from invited speakers about eye conditions and treatment, special devices for people with visual impairments, career information, and the like.

Whether the services of a rehabilitation teacher will be readily available to the 65,780 people who lose their sight each year is not certain. This dilemma is related to the average age of the typical newly blinded person and the amount of time needed to be an effective itinerant rehabilitation teacher. The fastest growing segment of the population with visual impairments is over sixty-five years of age, and most of these people will continue to receive instruction in their own homes on their own equipment rather than attend a comprehensive rehabilitation center, which is usually considered more suitable for young, vocationally bound clients. Therefore, the time it takes for the teacher to travel to the homes of students, along with the time necessary for record-keeping, will continue to influence the amount of time the teacher can spend with students. Records indicate that, if teachers visit each student every other week for one and a half hours and rely on family members and other volunteers to monitor progress in such areas as handwriting and sewing, the average newly impaired person will require one year to complete his or her program. Research and experience have shown that a rehabilitation teacher can complete teaching services with approximately 30 clients in a twelve-month period. To determine the number of teachers needed to serve the 65,780 people who will become blind in the United States each year, we divide by 30 and find that the number is 2,193. This translates into 97 teachers needed in the state of Illinois alone.

Determining the number of rehabilitation teachers needed is easier than determining the number actually available throughout the United States. According to estimates by experts in the field, there are between 500 and 700 teachers in the nation. Even if we arbitrarily double this to 1,400, this is still 793 fewer teachers than are necessary to serve the thousands of American citizens who lose their vision each year. The best advice to any person who becomes visually impaired is to get on an application list of an agency for the visually impaired as soon as possible. Fortunately, blindness usually progresses slowly, allowing the person to continue performing most activities at reduced efficiency until teaching services can be arranged. Finally, if it is necessary for a person's name to be put on a waiting list, most agencies will refer that person to another program such as the Regional Library for the Blind and Physically Handicapped, which provides recorded books at no cost to the patron.

The seven stories included in part 1 illustrate the tremendous variety of work performed by rehabilitation teachers and the spirit and commitment demonstrated by these highly trained professionals.

1

WHERE'S WILLIE?

Five o'clock Friday afternoon was the understood meeting time for those of us in the Carbondale, Illinois, area engaged in the rehabilitation of the blind. Without written notice or, in most instances, even a phone reminder, Bob Wright, Tom North, or I would swing through the front door of the Carbondale American Legion at about 5:15 P.M. and ask Wally, Pete, or whoever was tending bar if either or both of the others had arrived. Usually, the first one to roll in would order a round of beers, making sure to select the others' preferred brand, which would be set before them as soon as they mounted a bar stool. The unwritten agenda for these Friday get-togethers regularly included some friendly bantering among the patrons up and down the bar, a review of the major happenings around town during the week, and, at some point, a discussion of some aspect of rehabilitation practice that had occurred since last Friday's get-together. Often this discussion of the week's work would digress into the swapping of yarns and amusing incidents that we had experienced at some time during our careers in rehabilitation. It was during one of these Friday afternoon gatherings in the mid-1960s that Tom North, who was currently employed in the Business Enterprise Unit of the Illinois Division of Vocational Rehabilitation, recalled an experience during his tenure as a home teacher of the blind in the 1940s that involved a teenage blind girl who was so fearful that Tom was planning to place her in the residential School for the Blind in Jacksonville, Illinois, that she would hide out in the woods when he visited the home.

While Pete was setting up another round, Bob, who was the rehabilitation counselor for the blind in the southern sixteen counties of Illinois, told about the time a new client thought he was an eye doctor. The man had been referred by his doctor for financial assistance in purchasing eyeglasses. When Bob had completed the application for services, the client asked for his glasses. Although Bob had been reading the application in Braille and recording the answers with his Perkins Braille writer, the client had expected him to prescribe and fit the corrective lenses.

After Bob had finished his story, I recalled a strange encounter I had had with a student in the 1950s. Although my primary job duty at the time was the teaching of Braille, typing, homemaking, and other adjustment skills to newly blind persons in their homes, I was also responsible for maintaining talking book machines (phonographs provided by the Library of Congress to blind people for listening to books on long-playing records). An unscheduled maintenance check on one of these machines was the setting for my story.

Willie Jones resided in Ullin, a small settlement located on Route 51 about fifteen miles north of Cairo, Illinois. Visits to clients on Route 51 comprised one of the few trips each month for which I was permitted to use a car and driver, the most costly mode of transportation. In those days, rehabilitation teachers and other human service workers, blind or sighted, were required to travel by train or bus, but neither trains nor buses stopped in many of the small towns along Highway 51. Therefore, one or two times each month, a driver would pick me up about 8:00 A.M., and we would spend the day traveling to the homes of blind persons in the communities between Carbondale and Cairo for the purpose of teaching cane travel, Braille, cooking, and other subjects needing special methods and equipment for the blind. We also made annual visits to maintain talking book machines for patrons of the Library for the Blind, many of whom were former students.

At the time of this incident, Willie Jones was one of my former students who still received an annual talking book check. His teaching program had been completed about twelve months prior to this visit, at which time he was informed that he would be contacted each year for the purpose of inspecting his record player and making any minor repairs, such as tube and needle replacements.

As the driver shifted my 1953 Plymouth station wagon into first gear and eased out the clutch, I read the name on the top Braille card in the Union County address file and informed Fred that we would be making our first stop at the home of Nancy Williams in Cobden, about twenty miles south of Carbondale. My attention was then given to examining the notes on each student we were to visit that Friday morning. These lesson plan notes reminded me that Nancy would be learning to peel vegetables by touch, descend steps with a white cane, and read Braille; Jack Webb was going to take his first solo cane trip to the post office; and Beulah Bell would be working on a rug that she was weaving for her daughter's wedding gift. There were no notes for Willie Jones, who would be our second contact at about 11:00, because Willie was scheduled for a routine library check.

I stopped reading when Fred turned on the radio and Hank Williams's voice filled the car with "I'm So Lonesome I Could Cry." I lighted a Winston and began wondering how Willie was making out. He had been "at the bottom of the barrel," as he put it, when we had first met in 1957. He was referred by the County Department of Public Aid a few months after moving to southern Illinois from Memphis, Tennessee, where he had made his living playing the guitar and singing blues and country music. When he lost his sight from glaucoma, Willie's self-confidence left him. He stopped booking jobs and stayed in his apartment until his money was gone and his girlfriend, who had taken care of him "like a baby since my blindness," left him to return to her husband in Mississippi. Willie did the only thing he could think of: He swallowed his pride and asked some friends at a nightclub where he had worked last to take up a collection for his transportation to the home of his sister in Ullin, Illinois.

He had been sitting on the front steps of his sister's house, strumming a guitar and singing "I'm So Lonesome I Could Cry," when I got out of the car and introduced myself as the home teacher of the blind. In a rich tenor voice tinged with sadness, Willie offered me a seat on the steps and mused that the most valuable lesson he could learn was how to make money without his sight. He told his story, ending with his arrival at the home of Mary Mae Allan, his younger sister who lived in this house with her husband, Josh, and two children. He was not receiving Blind Assistance yet, and living off of his brother-in-law, who was working part time, was a drain on the family's meager resources.

After a lengthy interview on the actual barriers to Willie's resuming his employment as a musician, he had agreed to learn some alternate methods of compensating for his lost sight, such as using a white cane for foot travel, managing his money by folding bills differently according to denomination and feeling the differences among coins, and learning to write the chord sequences of new songs in Braille. In a series of biweekly visits over a twelve-month period, Willie learned enough of these skills to satisfy himself, and his teaching case was closed. At our last teaching session in the spring of 1958, he had reported that he was working three nights a week in a local night spot. The money wasn't near as much as he had made in Memphis, but he was able to contribute to the family income on a regular basis. Also, he had begun "keeping company with a nice widow lady I met at the Abyssinian Methodist Church," where he had begun singing in the choir. Overall, Willie felt his life was improving.

By the time I finished another Winston, we were crossing the bridge over the Illinois Central track at the north side of Cobden. Nancy Williams was waiting for me in her porch swing, so we began with the lesson on ascending her front porch steps by first checking the width and depth of the steps with the cane and then positioning the cane so that it pointed down at an angle from her right hand to contact the front edge of each step just beyond her left foot. When she reached the bottom, the cane could drop no further, notifying her that she had reached the last step. After practicing going up and down steps for about thirty minutes, we moved into Nancy's kitchen where she received instruction in peeling and dicing apples in preparation for mixing a Waldorf salad. This salad was to be a surprise for her husband, who had been performing the more dangerous cooking tasks, such as peeling and frying foods, since Nancy's visual loss.

We were back on the road by 10:00 A.M., and after stopping for coffee in Dongola, we pulled into Willie's sister's yard about 11:00 A.M. I was surprised when Fred said there were three other cars already parked in the yard, because Mary Mae and Josh had not owned an automobile when I had last visited in 1958. Walking up the front steps, I could hear several voices inside the house. I was greeted warmly by Mary Mae and offered a glass of Kool-Aid after being seated in a comfortable chair.

There seemed to be about six or seven people in the living room. I knew Mary Mae, Josh, and their two children, Rebecca and Daniel, and Mary Mae introduced me to the others, who were Willie's cousins. After some small talk about the nice weather and how well the fish were biting at Horse Shoe Lake, Mary Mae said she guessed I had come for the record player. I replied that I had really come to see Willie. In a somber voice Josh said that everyone present appreciated my visit and the help Willie had received from "the blind program." Acknowledging Josh's kind words with the statement that Willie was a good student who knew what he needed and applied himself to learn it, I said, "By the way—where is Willie?" Since we were talking about him, I assumed he was in the other room or had gone someplace with a friend or relative.

It was Mary Mae who spoke in a tearful voice. "He's right there beside you. You can touch his hand." And she took my hand and placed it on Willie's cold one. My shock at finding out that Willie was dead must have shown on my face because Mary Mae said they thought I had heard about Willie's heart attack and had been sent by the government to pick up the talking book machine.

I admitted that I was surprised and saddened by Willie's passing and went on to explain that I had only come to see if Willie was having any trouble with his machine or the Library for the Blind at Jacksonville. Josh informed me that Willie had complained of severe pain in his left arm shortly after breakfast the previous morning. He summoned a neighbor who transported Willie to St. Mary's Hospital in Cairo, where he was pronounced dead. After giving me another cup of Kool-Aid to settle my nerves, Mary Mae said they had seen my station wagon turn off the highway and decided that I had been notified of Willie's death and had come for the record player so some other blind person could have the use of it.

After the body had been prepared by the undertaker, Willie was laid out in his sister's living room, and other members of the family were notified. Relatives had begun arriving about six the previous afternoon, and, according to custom, they divided themselves into teams of two or three to sit beside Willie until the funeral, which would be Saturday afternoon. Mary Mae said that other relatives and friends, including Willie's former sweetheart, would arrive Saturday morning, and in the meantime, she and the other local relatives and friends would make sure that the body was not left unattended.

Again expressing my sincere sympathy to the relatives clustered in that small living room where the heat of the summer sun was moderated by the cool breeze drifting through the open windows and our words were accompanied by the songs of birds perched in the tall poplar trees in the yard, I accepted the talking book that Josh placed into the rear of the station wagon. As I closed the door and Fred started the Plymouth, I finally formulated the question that had been rattling around in my subconscious.

"Josh, you said Willie passed away yesterday morning. So why did Mary Mae assume I knew Willie had died before I got here?"

Josh's voice took on a confidential tone. "Well, Mr. Roberts, we all know the government has ways of finding out things, 'specially the Pension Department. Why, they seemed to know every time Willie or any of these old-age pensioners around here made a dollar because they would take it off of their checks. We figured the pension people called your office." I once more said that I had not been aware of Willie's passing until Mary Mae had made me aware of it. As Fred drove out of the yard, Josh said he hoped that whoever got Willie's machine would enjoy the talking books.

As I recall, the lessons with Jack and Mrs. Bell went well that Friday, but my thoughts kept returning to Willie—how he had made peace with his blindness, resumed his musical vocation, and even developed a relationship with "a nice widow lady." But Willie's life as a rehabilitated blind person had ended yesterday after breakfast with a severe pain in his left arm. I wondered if he had felt helpless and alone again at the end. That night, I spent some time listening to some old Hank Williams records, including "I'm So Lonesome I Could Cry," and thinking about Willie.

THE BRAILLE BIBLE

On a sunny afternoon in the spring of 1982, funeral ceremonies were completed for my friend L. D. "Jack" Norman, and the mourners were gathered in small groups around their cars engaged in quiet conversation. Dick Tauber, Tut Bollinger, Dick Swank, and the other pallbearers, all of us having been close personal friends as well as work associates of Mr. Norman, began recalling amusing experiences we had shared with Jack. Our reminiscences took my mind back to 1954 and the morning in Jack's office when he told me of one of his early experiences with the first rehabilitation teacher assigned to the Carbondale office of the Department of Public Welfare.

Jack, the first regional director of the Department of Public Welfare field offices, was responsible for approximately twelve social workers, two social work supervisors, four youth commission staff, and one home teacher of the blind, the position I was appointed to on January 1, 1954. Due to the technical nature of my work, my supervision was provided by I. N. Miller, who worked out of the Industrial Home for the Blind in Chicago, but I was responsible to Mr. Norman for routine administrative activity, which required one or two meetings each month to deal with such matters as expense accounts, cooperation with other local agencies, and public relations.

During one of these meetings, I placed my Braille list of discussion items on his desk, and we concentrated on the disposition of these items for about thirty minutes. Finally, he lighted a cigar and said, "You know, when I gave you a ride to the Illinois School for the Blind at Jacksonville the fall after your eighth grade graduation, I never thought about you completing college and working here. Why, when Heinz Adam asked me to take you to Jacksonville, he was not sure you would complete high school because you were determined to make your living as a musician."

Mr. Heinz Adam, my first rehabilitation teacher, was largely responsible for my choosing the same profession. Heinz first appeared at the Sight Saving Class, where I was a blind student trying to fit into a class in which the other students used large print, sometime during the 1944–45 school year. At first, I had difficulty understanding him because of his very pronounced German accent. As soon as he was able to make me understand that he had a system known as Braille that would enable me to read books myself (I had been depending on other students and my mother to read for me), I buckled down and learned to converse with Heinz in short order. He continued to show up for a Braille lesson each week until my graduation from grade school, by which time I was able to read a biography of John Gutenberg and take notes with a slate and stylus. Mr. Adam was the kind of teacher who seemed to know exactly what his students were capable of accomplishing, and he simply did not accept less from them.

Jack continued, "Yes, although Heinz was worried about your completing high school, he said he knew you were capable of completing college, and he was going to keep working on you until you were convinced that college was your best ticket to a good job. When he said that, I should have known that you would finish college, because Heinz never gives up when he decides on a course of action for one of his students. Well, that is, he almost never gives up. Let me tell you of the one time I knew Heinz to give up on a student." Jack relighted his cigar and began the following narrative.

Heinz was assigned to the newly created field office of the Department of Public Welfare located over the WCIL radio station in Carbondale in 1944. Having lived in Chicago since moving from Germany, he arrived in Carbondale to assume the position of home teacher of the blind with no experience in rural America but with boundless enthusiasm and energy. Having completed college and special courses in home teaching at Ypsilanti, Michigan, he began learning the more routine aspects of his job, including the routes of the Carbondale-Harrisburg Bus Company, which would enable him to visit students in the larger towns of Carmi, Cairo, Du Quoin, and Mt. Vernon. But, in the 1940s, a large percentage of the population resided on isolated farms accessible only by unpaved roads in dry weather. Heinz had to depend on his new boss, Jack Norman, or a social worker, who might be visiting clients nearby, for transportation to these isolated students.

One of these, Madge Underwood, lived with her husband about a mile west of a little settlement in Franklin County known as Bone Yard Woods. Madge was referred to the Division of Visitation of the Adult Blind by the Franklin County Department of Public Aid. Therefore, it was an easy matter to arrange for transportation to the Underwood farm on a more-or-less regular basis with the caseworker who called on aid recipients in the vicinity of Bone Yard Woods. In fact, it was Mrs. Underwood's public aid caseworker who first introduced Mr. Adam to her and her husband and persuaded Mr. Underwood that home teaching might enable his wife to resume some of the cooking and housekeeping, which would permit him to spend more time farming. So Heinz began making monthly visits to Madge Underwood for the purpose of teaching her such cooking techniques as peeling vegetables in water so that residual peeling would be easily perceived by touch, using the changing odors of foods to gauge doneness, and using nested measuring cups and spoons to determine the correct amount of ingredients in recipes. He augmented these cooking lessons with housekeeping techniques including sweeping floors in bare feet in order to feel any remaining dirt, dividing large areas into small sections that could be thoroughly cleaned and inspected by touch, and separating Mr. Underwood's colored socks for the laundry by pinning each pair together as soon as he took them off. Madge was also able to resume mending clothing by using needle threaders and other sewing techniques developed by teachers of the blind.

Once cooking, cleaning, and laundry methods were learned and Madge found she still had free time during the day when her husband was busy in the field, Heinz began reviewing the notes taken during his first visit in order to discuss hobbies and interests that Madge could resume for personal and spiritual enrichment. Having been accustomed to regular Bible reading and church attendance, she embarked on the study of Braille with enthusiasm. Mr. Underwood showed less acceptance for this phase of his wife's rehabilitation, saying that she had enough housework to keep her busy, but he made no strenuous objection, "as long as she can manage her housework without tiring herself out."

So, Heinz continued regular Braille lessons through the winter and spring except when the road to the Underwood farm was impassable because of snow, mud, or high water. It was mid-June when Jack Norman found Heinz waiting in his office one Monday morning with the request for assistance in delivering the Braille Bible, which had been shipped to the office from the American Bible Society. Jack had been planning a swing through Franklin County, so he readily agreed to drive by the Underwood farm, which was only two or three miles out of his way.

Jack did not become aware of the problem until he arrived at the office the following Monday to pick up Heinz and the Braille Bible. Parking his Studebaker coupe in front of the office, Jack opened the front door and was facing Heinz across three large boxes. Learning that these boxes contained the entire Bible, Jack explained that loading them into his coupe would be about as impossible as forcing a battleship into a box-car. Even if they could wedge the boxes into the single seat, there would be no room for passengers. They finally solved the problem by un-crating the nineteen large Braille volumes and squeezing ten into the trunk and wedging six behind the seat, which left Heinz holding three. Heinz apologized as the loaded car pulled into the line of traffic.

"Chack" (which was how Heinz pronounced Jack), "I would not have imposed on you this way if this Braille Bible had not been so vital to Mrs. Underwood's rehabilitation. You see, she is one of the most motivated Braille students I have met in southern Illinois, and all because she wants to read the Bible."

Jack said something encouraging like, "Whatever we can do to encourage our clients is a good investment," as he made a slow turn on to East Main in order not to shift the load of books behind his seat.

They covered the thirty-five miles to the turn-off leading to Bone Yard Woods and ultimately to the Underwood farm in fifty minutes. As Heinz directed Jack on to the rutted road lead-ing to the farm, Jack shifted the car into low gear and slowed to about five miles per hour so that the muffler would not be torn off. The motor stalled when they hit a rock where the road crossed a dry creek bed. Jack restarted the engine and slowly eased up the steep incline with the sound of metal grinding on rock underneath and low-hanging tree limbs beating on top, warning of possible damage to the car. After about ten minutes of inching forward in low gear, they pulled out of the trees into a clearing. Driving through a wire gate, which Heinz opened and closed behind the car to keep the cows from escaping, Jack parked the car in front of a very small house in need of paint-ing with one of the porch steps broken.

A pleasant-looking plump woman wearing a sunbonnet was seated in a porch swing cooling herself with a fan. Heinz intro-duced Jack and explained how he had been able to obtain an entire Braille Bible at no cost to Mrs. Underwood, who was lavish in expressing her appreciation. However, Jack noticed a change from happiness to concern in her expression as they carried volume after volume into the small living room filled with rocking chairs, a library table, a sewing machine, and a heating stove.

As Jack placed the last volumes in one of the rocking chairs, the table and sewing machine being stacked several feet high, they heard a team and wagon pull into the yard. Jack looked out the front door and saw a stocky man of about fifty years inspecting the numbers on his license plate. After a minute, he unhitched the team of sweaty, gray horses and disappeared with them around the house, probably to a barn for noon feeding, thought Jack. In a few minutes, they heard the back screen door slam, and the heavy-set man, who Heinz introduced as Mr. Herman Underwood, came through from the kitchen. He did not acknowledge the introduction but turned on Heinz with the question, "What in the name of hell is all this stuff you're carrying in here?"

Heinz began to explain that Mrs. Underwood wanted a Braille Bible so that she could resume her daily religious worship by reading the word of God firsthand. She would also be able to take her turn in reading Scripture in Sunday school by carrying selected volumes to church. As Heinz started to continue his explanation, the farmer tapped him on the chest with a forefinger. "I know you're might near blind," he said firmly, "but your buddy, here [pointing at Jack], can tell you that there's not a damn foot of empty space left in this house, let alone enough room for a wagon load of books."

When Heinz protested that the books had been provided free and shipped to Madge by a Christian organization, Herman said in a loud voice, "You'll have to take them to somebody that's got more room."

"How about this?" asked Heinz. "Let your wife keep the Bible until I come back, just to find out if you can fit it in somewhere. All the volumes don't have to be kept in one room, or even in the house, if you have a dry outbuilding."

"I told you," the farmer shouted as he began pitching the

volumes out the front door, "you're not leaving this damn mess to clutter up our house!"

"You can't do that!" Heinz protested. "That's a new Braille Bible, never opened until this morning."

Pitching another volume, which landed on top of Jack's car, the now red-faced Mr. Underwood yelled, "I don't give two hoots in hell if it's *Gone with the Wind*! This junk is not staying in my house." By this time Mrs. Underwood was crying and telling her husband that she would not have asked for the Bible if she had known it would take up so much space. It was at this point that Jack stepped into the situation, assuring the irate farmer that he and Heinz would return the Bible and apologizing to both him and his wife for any discomfort caused by Heinz's well-intentioned efforts to help Mrs. Underwood learn to live with her blindness.

After a little more conversation, Herman apologized for "flying off the handle," but said that Jack, being sighted, could certainly see how it would be impossible to store such a large collection of books in such a small house. He even assisted Jack and Heinz in wedging the last few books behind the car seat, assuring Heinz, as the car eased through the wire gate, that Madge had learned a lot about keeping house and that she wouldn't need any further help.

They rode down the hill into the trees in silence. The car again stuck on the rock in the creek bottom, but the absence of a loud roar from a ruptured muffler or an oil trail from a leaking oil pan seemed to indicate no permanent damage as they continued back to Route 37. After riding for several miles with his forehead resting on his right hand, Heinz finally broke the silence. "Well, Chack," he pronounced in a subdued voice, "you know, you can't help everybody." Jack suggested that they at least help themselves by stopping for a pleasant lunch on the square in Benton, after which they would just go on about their business of helping those who needed and wanted their services, which they proceeded to do for many more years.

THE MISSING PAGE

Blind since childhood, Raymond Dickinson brought his training in social work to his job as a home teacher of the blind in the early 1930s. Shortly after beginning employment, he became chairman of the Illinois Braille Committee, which produced the Illinois Braille Series of 1933. This book has been used throughout the world for teaching persons who become blind in adult life. Revised in 1952, 1960, and 1992, this text has enabled at least 100,000 blind persons to read and write Braille.

The first revision got underway in 1951 when Ray Dickinson had an 11:00 A.M. appointment with the three members of the Illinois Braille Committee. The women shown to the chairs arranged around his desk were the best Braille teachers on his staff and represented a wide range of personality, experience, and talent. Anna Johnson, the second rehabilitation teacher added to the staff following the creation of the home teaching program for the blind in 1911, was totally committed to improving the lives of her students. She was characterized by other teachers and students as a very prim and proper lady, who strove for perfection and expected others to do the same. Florence Horton, a recent graduate of Southern Illinois Normal

University at Carbondale, was a staff veteran of five years. A former student at the Illinois School for the Blind, she was a Braille expert and extremely capable in all areas of functioning without vision. Before joining the home rehabilitation teaching staff, Florence worked at the Illinois Industries for the Blind, a firm that employed blind people in the production of bed linens and other materials used by the armed services during World War II. Dorothy Dykema, the youngest and newest member of the staff, was an accomplished musician as well as an energetic teacher who was always anxious to try new teaching methods. Ray told himself that he had selected a committee with just the right mix of experience, education, values, and temperament to produce a 1952 revision of the Braille Series that would retain the high quality and relevance to the needs of the current group of students that had made the 1933 text so successful.

He outlined the committee's assignment, explaining the need to hold to the basic plan of the 1933 text with its emphasis on such study aids as the inclusion of raised print letters each time a new character was introduced. This self-help feature was vital because students were expected to study assignments independently between teacher home visits that occurred every two or three weeks.

A work plan was agreed upon: Each committee member would work independently on a particular section during two-week periods, and the full committee would meet at Anna's apartment every other Friday afternoon to iron out differences. The work was progressing well by the late spring of 1951. Several selections in the 1933 text that had been reprinted from elementary school readers had been replaced by stories taken from the Great American Series, which were more appropriate and interesting for adult students. Some minor regrouping of Braille contractions and the addition of a test had resulted in a slightly larger text.

By the Friday afternoon in late May when the committee encountered the strange phenomenon of the missing page, the final, perfect master copy of the completed 1952 Braille Series was being proofread. As usual, Florence arrived at Anna's apartment first because Dorothy had to travel all the way from the south side. The aroma of warm apple pie greeted Dorothy when Anna opened the door to the third-floor apartment. Announcing that Myrtle, Anna's roommate (who also happened to be blind), was baking an apple strudel for their afternoon tea, Anna showed Dorothy to a high-backed rocker, and the three teachers engaged in the proofing of the Braille text, each reading a selection while the others listened intensely for grammatical errors. The material had already been checked several times for spelling and punctuation errors as well as for the correct use of Braille contractions.

After this final reading, the book would be sent to the print shop at the School for the Blind in Jacksonville, where Louis Rodenberg, manager of the print shop, would use a heavy-duty Braille writer to copy the text on very thin lead plates, which would be used to press the dots into heavy paper. These lead plates could emboss three thousand copies before they became so flattened that the Braille was unreadable.

After working for about two hours, Anna asked Myrtle whether it was time to break for tea. Myrtle needed about ten more minutes, so Anna told Dorothy she would have time to proof the next selection. It was only one page, but it was very important; it was a composition by Superintendent Raymond Dickinson.

"It simply would not do to overlook an error in Mr. D's composition," Anna stated emphatically. Dorothy arranged the proof page on the board placed across the arms of her chair to keep the material flat and read very deliberately, carefully pronouncing each syllable. As the reading concluded, Myrtle announced, "Tea for four," and each person received a steaming cup and a warm serving of strudel. The next half hour was consumed with the exchange of news about each member's life since the last meeting.

When the break was over, the manuscript was passed to Florence, who was to continue the reading. "Did you plan to re-check that last piece?" Florence inquired.

"I gave everything to you," Dorothy answered.

"Not everything," replied Florence. "That piece by Mr. Dickinson isn't here."

Dorothy frantically searched her briefcase where she had placed the manuscript during the tea break. The others also checked their materials for the missing page.

"It just has to be there, Florence!" Dorothy said.

"I don't know what happened to it unless you ate it with your strudel, but it is not here," responded Florence, a tinge of irritation in her usually pleasant voice. The blind women continued to search, checking the bookcase, coffee table, chairs, and even the kitchen counter, just in case Myrtle had somehow folded the missing page into the dessert dishes when she carried them to the kitchen.

When they had exhausted their ideas for places to look, the ladies sat in silence, except for the rhythmic rocking of Dorothy's chair. It was Anna that startled the group by commanding, "Dorothy! Move your chair away from the wall. The rocker is tearing the wallpaper." Dorothy maintained that she was not near the wall, which caused Anna to kneel behind her chair and feel for herself. "Stand up!" she ordered, and when Dorothy complied, Anna removed the missing page, which had been crumpled beyond recognition, from beneath the rocker.

After everyone tried unsuccessfully to decode the Braille characters from the mutilated paper, Anna announced that there was only one thing to do. Under no circumstances could they tell the boss they had destroyed his composition, so they must complete the tedious process of re-embossing the page. This involved locating the faint impressions on the crumpled page and re-perforating them with a stylus. Following some quick calculation, Dorothy, who knew she would be the one to redo the page, asked Anna, "Do you realize that there are approximately seven hundred dots on a Braille page?" After further consideration of the time and effort required to reconstruct the composition, Dorothy still decided that she would rather redo the page than explain the situation to Mr. Dickinson.

Whether the composition was totally correct was difficult to determine. At least, the author never mentioned any errors to the members of the Illinois Braille Committee who gathered at Anna Johnson's apartment on that balmy May afternoon almost forty-five years ago.

4

The Rehabilitation of
Robert Ingersol

Many times during my forty years of teaching newly blind people the skills to reestablish their productive, independent lives, I have wondered who, among the thousands of my blind acquaintances, has made the most successful adjustment to the loss of eyesight. The blind underwater diver who engaged in contract salvage of materials from sunken barges on the Ohio River? He certainly had an unusual occupation. The man blinded from a chemical accident who learned Braille in three lessons and then refused to use this system because he could no longer read several hundred pages in an evening? The young woman who became blind in her last year at medical school? Through sheer willpower, hard work, and assertiveness, she completed her education and became a practicing physician. Or was it the college professor who mastered Braille, typing, and mobility in four months with only three hours of rehabilitation teaching each Friday afternoon? This highly motivated professor never interrupted his teaching schedule to attend a rehabilitation center, insisting on fitting his training into his regular routine, and, after the completion of his program, he continued publishing articles in professional journals, eventually becoming chairman of his department.

Each of these people was remarkable in facing blindness head-on and learning the necessary skills and strategies to carve out a life-style of his or her own choosing. However, there is one person in my memory who was bigger than life, even though he weighed only 135 pounds and stood five feet five inches tall before arthritis fused his hip joints, leaving him stooped so that his legs and trunk formed a ninety-degree angle.

I was first introduced to Bob Ingersol and his wife, Edith, by my rehabilitation teacher, Heinz Adam, in 1946. The stated reason for dropping by the Ingersol home that afternoon in late April was for me to hear Bob's talking book machine, a record player on which he "read" books on subjects ranging from philosophy to wild West fiction. If I liked what I heard, Heinz said he would arrange for me to borrow one of these machines from the Library of Congress, which also provided the recorded books.

Looking back on that visit, I think Heinz had a much more important reason for introducing me to Bob. I was having difficulty accepting Heinz's ideas about my going to high school and possibly even college, and I think he wanted me to become acquainted with Bob in order to see for myself just how far a person could go in overcoming the limitations of blindness. Like me, Bob was blind, but he was also severely crippled. Yet, it soon became apparent that Bob lived a fuller life than most people, even though he seldom traveled farther than the few feet to the dinette or to his bedroom. He had five assets that brought the world and the people in it to him, since he could not go out to them: his radio, his talking book machine, his typewriter, his telephone, and (most importantly) his personality.

Not having known Robert Grant Ingersol prior to his becoming totally blind and orthopedically disabled, I cannot comment extensively on the development of his charismatic personality. According to his wife and several of his adolescent peers, Bob's capacity to impress and influence people was evident many years prior to his disability. Perhaps the most convincing evidence that he possessed those traits is that his friends and associates, sighted and blind, actually lost their awareness of his physical impairments when they were interacting with him.

Bob had a clear, resonant voice that exuded friendliness, and he was able to project his speech in such a manner that he seemed to be looking straight at his listener, although he was unable to see whether the lights were on or off. Bob was able to keep informed of local and world affairs by listening to the radio and the reading of newspapers by Edith and the female college students who rented spare rooms in the Ingersol house. He read more than a hundred books each year on a wide range of subject matter, enthusiastically sharing his acquired knowledge and life experience with friends, such as his student renters, who were doing school assignments or trying to cope with life's challenges and problems. Many of the people who benefited from Bob's wisdom during their college years kept in contact with him until his death in 1972. Although a slow typist, Bob regularly wrote letters filled with news, humor, and advice to friends located throughout the United States.

Another characteristic that endeared Bob to his friends was his sense of humor. He enjoyed practical jokes, either on himself or on one of us. A favorite prank involved a short range radio transmitter that Bob had ordered from a catalog. When someone who did not know about the transmitter was visiting, Bob would excuse himself and go into his bedroom. An accomplice, Edith or one of his friends who had been the victim of this prank, would turn on the radio for the stated purpose of catching the weather forecast or the news. Bob would then interrupt the current program to transmit a bulletin announcing that the unsuspecting guest had just won the Irish Sweepstakes or some other astounding information. Of course, we would enlighten the guest before any harm was done, and everyone would have a good laugh.

Considering Bob's enjoyment of practical jokes, it seems fitting that his rehabilitation was, to some extent, due to a joke played on him by his rehabilitation teacher, A. P. Gillick. Pop Gillick, as he was known, became a home teacher of the blind in the early 1930s, when the qualification for this position was only a high school diploma. Although Pop did not have the advantage of college psychology courses, he was a master at sizing up people. His questioning of those who knew Bob, coupled with his knowledge of human behavior, seem to have provided the necessary insight to develop a strategy for jump-starting Bob into overcoming the anger and depression that were impeding his adjustment to blindness.

Pop was able to piece together a general sketch of Bob's life prior to the onset of his disabilities and conclude that he had been a rather successful young man. Bob had completed one year of high school and worked as a yard clerk for the Illinois Central Railroad. He had spent some time in the U.S. Navy, after which he married Edith Fallon and began working for his father, a painting contractor. Bob must have been a crackerjack painter and wallpaper hanger, because he was still advising people on color matching and wall covering techniques twenty years after he became totally blind.

Only four years after his marriage in 1921, Bob began experiencing the crippling effects of rheumatoid arthritis. Although he became unable to work, he was able to drive his car until the mid-1930s. He and Edith spent much time fishing and just driving about to visit with friends and see the countryside, which diverted his mind from his inability to earn the money for keeping up his and Edith's living standard. However, when he lost his sight in 1935, Bob said he totally gave up trying, spending as much time as possible in bed. Based on this brief sketch, Mr. Gillick concluded that Robert G. Ingersol was a very sociable man who enjoyed action, learning, and earning money to provide for himself and his wife, whom he loved.

With this much information, Mr. Gillick felt he could convince Bob to begin learning to do such things as eat without accidents, get about in his home, read Braille, and, perhaps, acquire some skill or product that could provide income to supplement his wife's earnings from renting rooms to college students. The only problem encountered by A. P. was that Bob would not come out of his bedroom to talk to him. After spending time talking to Mrs. Ingersol on two home visits, he simply asked her to show him the way to Bob's bed. Gillick located the bed with his cane and said, "Stick out your hand, brother, and shake hands with another blind man."

Here, we pick up the story from Bob, as he told it to me many years later. He said this big, happy-sounding man plopped down on his bed and felt around until he found his hand, which he shook vigorously while keeping up a running commentary on the beautiful weather, Bob's good fortune in having such a pretty wife, and how wonderful it was to be alive. Bob said his first thought was that any blind person who thought life was worth living and acted as happy as this guy had to be crazy. Therefore, he decided to humor him long enough to end the visit and to instruct Edith never to let him in the house again. Reasoning that, being a state employee, his visitor's pay might be based on the number of people who listened to his pitch about all the things he could teach them, Bob felt it would be unkind to refuse to listen to this poor blind man, who, after all, needed any money he could get to provide for his family.

Bob withdrew his hand from the grip of his visitor and made himself as comfortable as possible to endure the presentation. It wasn't as easy as he thought. The man kept asking him questions such as whether he would like to learn to read again, write on a typewriter, or build birdhouses, with Bob answering negatively to all inquiries. When the fellow finally ran out of questions, Bob had one for him.

"What's that strange sound you keep making, kind of like a piece of fishing line being pulled through a ring or loop?" A. P. informed Bob that he was using leather lacing to assemble a wallet and asked if Bob would like to try it. "What would I do with a wallet if I could make one? I don't have any money to put in it," Bob responded.

"Putting money in blind folk's pockets is part of my job," Pop laughed. "You see, home teachers not only teach blind people, they also help them get into some kind of paid work if possible."

"Do you expect me to believe that you can fix things so a blind man can earn money in the middle of the worst depression in history?"

The tone of Bob's question must have conveyed a subtle shift away from absolute rejection of the services offered up to this point, for Pop played a hunch. "It's sort of like that. You see, we have to give the blind folks a little edge, so we have arranged for them to be the only people who can sell these blind-made products," Pop explained. He was being a little misleading, but he knew he would probably lose any further opportunity to help this alert, resourceful individual if he did not leave the interview with a ray of hope for improving his financial situation. Besides, it was his job to develop employment for persons who were blind, and there were some organizations in large cities that marketed products made by blind people. No doubt, he could arrange the sale of a few items to keep Bob motivated until success rebuilt a little self-confidence. The Vocational Rehabilitation Program for the Blind was not established until after World War II, but in the 1930s the rehabilitation teachers were charged with providing employment for people who were blind. Pop had successfully assisted a number of these people in establishing small businesses, such as the manufacture and sale of brooms, furniture repair, and assembling birdhouses for sale, but he was not convinced he could find a project that Bob could do successfully because of his orthopedic impairment.

Well, he would have to cross that bridge when he came to it. Right now, he had to get Bob going on something that would build his self-confidence, so they spent the next hour working on assembling a wallet, which Bob learned quickly, displaying good hand dexterity in spite of his arthritis.

Before leaving that afternoon, Pop had a stroke of good luck. He learned that one of the student renters had a sister employed at a factory near East St. Louis, where Pop's office was located. He arranged with the sister to order some items from Bob, who would be learning to make these items during the next few months. This would provide the income he had promised Bob.

Even Pop was surprised at Bob's success. The sister of Bob's student renter and her friends bought more than eight hundred dollars worth of items. By the time these sales began to drop off, Bob was learning to cane chairs, and his many contacts throughout southern Illinois enabled him to obtain more chair reseating than he could do. As a result, he even had to train an assistant to keep up with the volume of work during the 1950s. This freed up the necessary time for Bob to maintain his business records with the use of Braille and typing, which he had also learned from Mr. Gillick.

As the years passed and Bob became more successful and influential, he often joked about the trick used by Pop Gillick to get him started on the road of adjustment to blindness. He would end the story by saying, with a chuckle in his voice, "By the time I found out that blind people didn't have a monopoly on the sale of leather goods, I had already made a little money and had decided that blindness wasn't so bad after all."

That Bob Ingersol was able to successfully operate a home business requiring continuous physical effort and manual skill without sight and with severe physical limitations imposed by arthritis is truly remarkable. What is miraculous is the degree to which he was able to overcome the stereotyped images of blindness in the perceptions of the hundreds of Southern Illinois University graduates, who knew him in his capacity as a landlord, and other friends who periodically contacted him for advice, emotional support, and fellowship throughout his life.

5

Color Blind

At a colleague's retirement party in 1992, I bumped into Louis Davis, who had joined the Illinois Service for the Blind in 1953 when I was an intern at the old Industrial Home for the Blind in Chicago. Since Louis had been an intern the previous year, he had gone out of his way to help me with some of the routines involved in the daily practice of rehabilitation teaching, and we have remained friends during the succeeding forty years.

Lou greeted me with one of those magic phrases that evoke a snapshot memory of a shared experience. "Have you shaken up the old establishment lately?" he asked. As we exchanged a few pleasantries and brought each other up to date on personal events, my mind lingered on the memory his question had evoked, and I continued to savor this long-past experience until the party was over and I was drifting off to sleep.

The situation that Lou's greeting brought to mind had occurred on a warm summer evening in 1956. The week before, the switchboard operator had notified me that I had a long distance call from Chicago. Louis Davis was on the line telling me the good news that he would be attending the two-week rehabilitation seminar offered by Southern Illinois University. Although he would be staying on campus and attending class from 8:00 A.M to 4:00 P.M, including Saturday, Louis hoped we could get together for dinner and a few drinks. I jumped at the chance to return some of the kindness Lou had extended when I had been serving my internship far from my hometown of Carbondale. Lou had invited me to several social activities, which enriched my four-month residency in the Windy City. I assured him that a night on the town in Carbondale would be an interesting experience. We agreed that I would meet Louis at his dorm on Friday evening following his arrival, and we would take a walking tour of the restaurants and bars.

Between Louis's phone call and our anticipated night on the town, I told several acquaintances at such local watering holes as Bill's Tavern, the Long Branch, John's Cafe, and the Rat Hole that I would be introducing them to a teacher of the blind from Chicago who had been instrumental in helping me succeed in my internship. As Louis and I made the rounds that Friday evening, the hospitality exceeded my expectations. Several bartenders set up free drinks, and many of the Carbondale natives shook hands with Lou and asked him about his work. These congenial encounters often ended with the locals affirming that, if Lou was a friend of mine, he was a friend of theirs.

We polished off the evening with an excellent dinner at the Hub Cafe. Again, the owner of this establishment rolled out the red carpet, seating us at a large table in a corner where he said we could enjoy our food undisturbed. Having spent most of the evening greeting and swapping yarns with others, we appreciated the opportunity to discuss work and personal matters. Lou told of an amusing incident involving Bruce McKenzie, our downstate supervisor of rehabilitation teachers. It seems that Bruce, who was from Kentucky and a country music fan, heard Louis, a highly trained classical vocalist, perform at the Illinois Federation of the Blind banquet. As Louis completed his rendition of several classical selections and stepped off the platform, Bruce grasped his hand and said, "Louis, you did a great job of singing! Why, if you keep practicing, you'll be as good as Ernest Tubb, the Texas Troubadour." While we were speculating about how Louis would sound with a country band, the steaks came, and we spent several minutes quietly enjoying our meal.

Over coffee and cognac, the conversation turned to the seminar Louis was attending and its relevance to the practice of rehabilitation teaching of the blind. He said there was a lot of emphasis being placed on the necessity of assisting newly disabled persons in coming to terms with their disability and gearing the rehabilitation program to the intrinsic motivation of the client. Developing resources to enhance the client's rehabilitation within his or her circle of friends and associates had also been discussed. One lecturer, a Mr. Porter from Washington, D.C., had complimented the field of work for the blind for leading the entire rehabilitation of the disabled movement in the development of techniques for teaching activities of daily living, such as identifying coins by texture and size and using Braille labels for identifying foods and medicines.

As we were settling our bill, Nick, the restaurant owner, rushed up to ask if our food had been tasty and the service satisfying. Ambling back to Louis's dorm, I suggested he join me for dinner at the Hub Cafe more often because of the VIP treatment we had received. I mentioned that my usual encounter with the staff of the Hub consisted of the necessary verbal exchange to learn what was on the menu, place my order, and pay the bill. Why, we were even assigned a quiet corner table away from the noise and conversation of the other diners. Lou joked that the restaurant staff recognized a sophisticated man from Chicago and were trying to make a good impression. Our talk continued in a lighthearted manner until we parted in front of Louis's dorm and I returned to my apartment.

Because the weekend was routine—cleaning the apartment, cooking and eating, catching up on reading and writing personal letters—I was out bright and early Monday morning. Leaving for the office an hour early, I stopped by Wastella's Cafe for a breakfast of biscuits and gravy. When the bill was paid and I was closing the front door behind me, Wastella said, "Be careful, and don't cause too much trouble."

My next stop was Bart's shoe-shine stand in Ray's Jewelry

Store. Beyond giving the best shoe shine in town, Bart was a source of information about the political and social activities and intrigues in Jackson County. He resided in Murphysboro, the county seat, and was a member of several activist groups, such as the NAACP. As he deftly snapped the rag to create a shine, which he said would reflect the images of the garter belts worn by the coeds I passed on the street, he filled me in on the progress of his nephew who had been a classmate of mine at Southern Illinois University. Handing back the quarter change from a half-dollar, Bart slapped me on the back and said, "Keep up the good work for the cause, brother."

"What cause?" I wondered, closing the door and walking toward my next stop, Walgreen's Drugstore, across the alley from my place of employment. Accepting thirty-five cents for a pack of Winston cigarettes, Tom, the proprietor, said my business was greatly appreciated and that he hoped my friends and I would continue patronizing his store. I thought this was a rather odd remark, but it was possible that Tom's poor hearing caused him to misunderstand something I said, so I assured him that he had my business as long as his store remained open.

Anticipating a cheerful greeting from Doris, our reception-ist, I was surprised to hear the voice of Katie, the office man-ager: "Mister Norman wants to see you in his office immedi-ately." She separated and emphasized the first syllable of the regional administrator's name so that it sounded like "Misss Ternorman." When Katie talked like this, it meant that Jack Norman had something serious on his mind.

Jack was one of the calmest, most in-command administra-tors I have ever known, and an urgent summons to his office indicated real trouble. When he closed the door, something he rarely did during routine business conferences, my throat be-gan to feel dry and the office, which was air conditioned, seemed unusually warm. Jack lighted a cigar, leaned back in his large swivel chair, and said, "It seems like you got some people ex-cited around here this weekend."

Since I had not left my apartment except for a trip to the corner grocery store, I said that my contact with people had been practically nonexistent over the weekend. Jack explained that he had received several phone calls, including one from a member of the Carbondale City Council, regarding my activities of the previous Friday evening. This really confused me because I had spent a quiet evening dining with a colleague from Chicago and taking him to a few neighborhood bars. I told Jack that it was difficult to see how such bland activity could excite the city fathers.

Jack took a long pull on his Dutchmaster cigar and drawled, "Well, you see, it really wasn't the activity that stirred up the community. It was your friend. Did you know he was a Negro?"

"Yes," I replied. "At least, he says he is a Negro, but, you know, black and white don't have a hell of a lot of meaning to a blind man. Besides, Louis Davis is a professional colleague of mine, and the least I can do when a fellow teacher comes to town is treat him to dinner and a few drinks."

Jack's voice became apologetic, "Don't get me wrong. I'm not implying that you should not extend courtesy to professional colleagues, black, white, or yellow, but there have been some meetings around here at which the idea has been discussed of boycotting restaurants and other businesses that discourage black folks from coming in. The people who called me were not riled up so much about you bringing a black person into the Hub Cafe as about your possible intentions. Someone heard Louis say that he is from Chicago and concluded that you had teamed up with an outside civil rights organizer to create an incident to provoke the boycott."

Explaining that I had no ulterior motive, that my sole intention was to welcome a friend and professional colleague to my town, I concluded, "Since I don't actually see people, I tend to identify them more by their vocations, ideas, and manners than by color. To me, Louis is a friend, a teacher, and a musician."

Jack took several puffs on his cigar and said, "That's amazing. You guys are not only blind, you're color blind. Maybe that's one of the few advantages of being blind—accepting people according to their accomplishments rather than their skin color. If seeing people had your advantage, maybe there wouldn't be any racial prejudice." He went on to say that he would convey my explanation to the concerned merchants and city fathers who would, no doubt, be greatly relieved and cease any further inquiries.

Of course, subsequent social activism and civil right legislation brought about the integration of the entire business establishment, but Lou and I can still reminisce about how we were pioneers in the integration of Carbondale without even realizing it until Jack Norman explained it.

6

THE EQUAL OPPORTUNITY ROBBERS

I feel fortunate to have attended a residential school where shared experiences and aspirations naturally resulted in friendships that have endured over the past forty years. Of the forty or so high school students who attended the Illinois School for the Visually Impaired between 1946 and 1950 (formerly the Illinois School for the Blind), at least twenty of us have remained in close contact.

On New Year's Eve in 1991, several of us former students, with our spouses, gathered at the home of Bob and Norma Wright to ring in the new year and renew our bonds of friendship. A heated discussion began to build over whether blind people are more vulnerable to robbery and assault than sighted people. Someone offered the opinion that criminals might tend to give blind people a break because they would feel guilty for attacking victims who could not see to defend themselves. Another guest wondered if criminals might tend to rule out blind victims because of the generally known fact that at least seventy percent of the blind population is unemployed and, therefore, are unprofitable prospects for robbery. Cathy, my wife, vehemently disagreed with the previous speakers, pointing out that she and I had been attacked by a mugger who forcibly took my wallet containing eighty dollars and two credit cards.

This interjection of a personal encounter with a criminal shifted the focus of conversation; now the group began to re-call situations in which blind people had been selected as victims by criminals. Helen Huddleston related a case in which a rap-ist testified at his trial that he chose a blind victim because he believed she could not identify him in court.

After refreshing our drinks and passing around a dish of hot popcorn, Bob told of an experience with a would-be robber just before Christmas of 1990. He had taken a bus to a downtown Decatur bank to withdraw travel funds for a trip to Chicago the following day. He placed the two hundred dollars in his inside coat pocket before leaving the bank lobby to board a city bus for the three-mile ride to his home. Arriving at the bus stop several minutes before the bus was due, Bob pulled up the col-lar of his London Fog coat to protect himself from the wind and blowing snow. Leaning against a post, which blocked a little of the biting wind, he was approached by a young-sound-ing man who announced that he had a weapon and demanded money. Noticing that there were no other voices near, Bob decided that yelling for help might be futile and could cause the man to attack him. Thinking quickly, as Bob usually did, he turned to the robber and asked in a voice filled with conde-scending sarcasm, "Now, just why in the hell do you think I would be standing here in the cold waiting on a bus if I had enough money to take a taxi?"

Tensing his muscles in readiness for self-defense, just in case his antagonistic question provoked physical violence, Bob ex-tended his opened hand containing the bus coins and continued, "I've walked home in the cold before, so take the damn bus fare if you're so hard up."

"That's really all you've got?" complained the robber.

Feeling he was gaining control of the situation and hearing a diesel motor, which was probably the bus approaching, Bob reinforced the assailant's growing belief that bus fare was the only bootie to be taken with the question, "Have you ever heard of a rich blind man?"

"Screw you!" the voice puffed into Bob's face, along with a

cloud of cigarette smoke. The sound of the bus door opening just behind him alerted Bob that now was the most opportune time to act. Unless he was totally irrational, the robber probably would not harm him with the bus driver and passengers as witnesses. Hoping that he would not be stabbed or shot in the back, Bob turned around, located the bus steps with his cane, and boarded. He felt his entire body relax when the door closed behind him.

"First seat on your left," advised the driver as he began moving the bus away from the curb. When the bus had merged into the line of moving vehicles and Bob was seated next to the door on the long bench reserved for the elderly and handicapped, the driver glanced at him and remarked, "It sure was nice of your friend to help you to the bus stop and wait with you until you boarded."

John Robinson asked Bob how the driver responded when he learned that the man waiting with Bob was trying to rob him. "I figured the driver would waste an hour or more with a useless investigation, so I just said that good friends are hard to find and started listening to my radio."

After bringing in more wood for the fire, Bob continued. "I thought I heard someone mention something about Don McBride getting robbed in East St. Louis way back in the sixties. Does anybody know the particulars?"

Dave Gentry said that, since I had been Don's supervisor at the time, I should be the best source for this story. I accepted a fresh can of Old Milwaukee from Bob and began to tell how Don McBride encountered a robber, mugger, or beggar (Don never was sure which) one cold afternoon in the early 1960s.

Don McBride moved to East St. Louis from Oklahoma with his wife and two small children in 1963 to accept the position of rehabilitation teacher of the blind for southwestern Illinois. His office was located in a five-story bank building on the busy corner of Fifth Street and Missouri Avenue. Because he provided counseling and instruction to newly blinded persons in their homes, Don usually spent only one full day in his office writing progress reports, making lesson plans, and doing other office work; the other four days of the week were spent providing instruction in Braille, typing, and cooking and administering other services to students throughout a ten-county area.

A significant number of these students resided in East St. Louis neighborhoods where reports of burglary and robbery were common. Although large of stature—six feet three and 240 pounds—Don expressed a fear of being attacked by an armed assailant while traveling by bus to teach students in dangerous neighborhoods. As he explained, "I'm not afraid of hand-to-hand combat, because I'm bigger than most people, but a blind man is not very effective against a knife or a gun." Having participated in wrestling at the Oklahoma School for the Blind and having been involved in other physical combat during his youth, Don knew he could hold his own when the other combatants relied only on hands and feet to inflict injury; however, a bullet or some other missile could come from any direction and cause mortal injury with no warning. So Don was always tense when traveling in areas where the crime rate was high, but he did not feel this tension as much in the downtown area around his office.

On Monday, Don's regular office day, his vague uneasiness about becoming a crime victim became a clear and present danger. Just as he finished packing his briefcase with the week's teaching supplies and was heading for the elevator at the end of the workday, the receptionist announced "an urgent call for Mr. McBride." Returning to his office, Don became engaged in a long-distance counseling session with a newly blinded client whom he had seen the previous Friday. This man apparently had become depressed over the weekend, and it took almost an hour to reassure him that learning such skills as typing, Braille, and cane travel could enable him to resume his life-style and accomplish his goal of reemployment.

By the time Don reached the elevator, there seemed to be no one left in the building. However, when he reached Missouri Avenue, it seemed to be populated with Christmas shoppers. Many were apparently burdened with packages, according to the rustling sounds of paper.

Don stopped near the alley and placed his briefcase on the walk in preparation for the ten-minute wait for the next scheduled bus. As he waited, the shopping crowd seemed to thin out, although there were still people entering and leaving the surrounding stores. He suddenly became aware that someone was standing very close to him. Just as Don started to step aside to make way for the newcomer, a man's voice spoke very near his left ear.

"Listen, blind man," he almost whispered, "I'm not going to hurt you, but I need money." The impression of being stabbed and shot at the same time overwhelmed Don, and with a pure reflex action, he dropped the white cane from his right hand and swung his fist with 240 pounds of force at the quiet voice. At the same instant, Don began shouting, "Help! Call the police! I'm being robbed!"

As people began to gather around, a reassuring voice, which Don recognized as belonging to the cigar store proprietor, said, "You're okay, Don. Whoever was bothering you has gone." Handing Don his cane and briefcase, the proprietor turned to the gathering spectators and asked if anyone had seen what happened. A lady with several packages spoke tentatively.

"I didn't see the beginning, only the end when the man got hit, but it looked like he was more in need of help than the blind man." She had seen Don drop his cane and strike the man who had been talking with him squarely in the mouth. The man appeared to skid along the alley as though propelled by a strong wind for about fifteen feet, then regained his balance and ran behind a building, leaving behind a few drops of blood.

Making sure that the assailant had not taken anything and that Don was not injured (except for the cut on his right knuckle, probably caused by the assailant's teeth), the cigar store owner told the crowd he would make sure Don made his bus connection without further difficulty. As the spectators drifted away and Don prepared to board his bus, a small boy pressed a tiny, hard object in his hand. "You sure nailed that guy," the child announced reverently. "I thought you might like to have one of his teeth. I found it in the alley." Don thanked the boy and boarded his bus for the thirty-minute ride home.

As the bus slowly worked its way up State Street, opening and closing its automatic doors at each corner to pick up or discharge passengers, Don kept wondering what were the true intentions of the quiet-spoken man whose tooth he held in his palm. Certainly, there had been no threat either in the voice or manner. In fact, the man had assured him that he intended no physical injury. Well, Don thought, continuing to ponder the man's intentions and the appropriateness of the response could not alter the situation. Don closed his mental examination of the incident with the comforting thought that, if he had encountered a robber, his quick, reflex action had preserved both his health and his money.

"That was a great story," Bryce Huddleston pronounced. "Can't you just see McBride belt that guy? Why, that's as good as the account of the girls being robbed in St. Louis." "The girls" were Cathy, my wife, Carol, John's wife, and Helen, Bryce's wife. The trio insisted that the McBride story was much better than the account of their robbery at the Steel Guitar Convention in St. Louis, but it was decided that each person in the group should have the opportunity to judge the merits of both stories. Cathy was elected to read their tale, which I had had published in the winter 1989 issue of the *Illinois Braille Messenger*. Norma brought the issue from a bookcase.

"I'll be right back!" Cathy shouted into my right ear over the music of a steel guitar and the stage band. "I'm going to take Helen and Carol to the restroom," she continued.

Helen and Carol were two of the five totally blind people attending the Steel Guitar Convention held every Labor Day weekend at the Clarion Hotel in St. Louis. The other totally blind persons in the group were Carol's husband, John, Bob, and I. My wife, Cathy, is partially sighted, having enough vision to read and travel unassisted by special travel devices or sighted guides.

As the three women filed out to the ladies' room, Bryce, Helen's husband, handed out cold beers from the cooler resting on the floor between him and Bob, and we all settled back to enjoy Herb Wallace and the band play several tunes from Herb's newest album. When he finished these selections about thirty minutes later, John mused, "I wonder if them girls got lost or ran away with some of them fancy guitar pickers from Nashville?"

While the next act was setting up equipment on the stage, someone tapped me on the shoulder. Cathy's tense voice whispered, "We have a problem. We've been robbed in the ladies' room!"

Everyone adjourned to the ladies' room upon hearing this news. When Cathy approached the restroom area, a security guard shouted, "Lady, your friends won't let us in the bathroom! Can you help?"

Cathy quickly explained that she had advised the other victims to lock the door behind her when she left the restroom before the five-minute waiting period ordered by the robber. She then accompanied the guard to the door and assured their friends that it was safe to open up.

The next hour was spent by the security people taking down statements from each of the victims as to their exact memory of the incident and the items they had lost. Then, we all returned to Bob and Norma's room for a nightcap and a little unwinding. As the gathering broke up, someone said that the robber had not shown any mercy for the blind. John joked, "Blind people say they want to be treated just like everybody else. So, look at it this way; you folks encountered an equal opportunity robber."

When Cathy finished reading, the guests were still divided in their opinions of which was the better tale. It was generally agreed that a fair judgment would be possible only if I committed the McBride story to paper. This has now been accomplished, and the two stories, along with Bob's narrative of his experience with the robber in front of the bank, are here presented for all to judge their comparative merits.

7

BEYOND THE CALL OF DUTY

I was in Wichita, Kansas, in the early 1980s, catching up on developments in work for the blind since the last Mid-America Conference of Rehabilitation Teachers. I was with Bob, a rehabilitation teacher employed by the Kansas Agency for the Blind, when a pleasant female voice asked, "Bob, is that you?"

Responding in the affirmative, he introduced the newcomer to me as Jane Frost, "The famous rehabilitation teacher from Hays, Kansas." Now, the historical particulars of this story have faded from my memory, as has the real name of this young woman, but the intense emotions of suspense, fear, and admiration that her tale created in me have remained vivid.

To my inquiry about the source of Ms. Frost's fame, Bob expressed surprise that I had not heard of her on the evening news that past winter. He went on to explain that he had invited Jane to dinner to get a firsthand account of what had happened. Jane readily agreed to my becoming the third dinner partner.

Once we were seated in the hotel dining room and had finished ordering from the Braille menu prepared especially for our convention, Jane, an attractive young woman about thirty years old who spoke in a pleasant, clear voice with no noticeable ethnic or geographical accent, shared a brief sketch of her life up to the day she had encountered the blizzard that had changed her life. Having a history of congenital glaucoma, which had been controlled by medication, Jane's vision failed rapidly during her senior year in college, where she received a B.S. in education. By the time of our dinner engagement, her sight was limited to light perception, although she continued wearing glasses from habit, she said.

Encountering difficulty in obtaining employment as a public school teacher, Jane finally was persuaded by her rehabilitation counselor from the Missouri Bureau for the Blind to spend several months at Lions' World, an adjustment training center for the blind in Little Rock, Arkansas, where she learned homemaking methods for blind people, Braille, typing, and cane travel. While in training, Jane learned of an opening for an itinerant rehabilitation teacher in Hays, Kansas. With some additional training in such areas as psychological impact of blindness, she was able to secure this position and moved to Hays.

Within a year of Jane's acceptance of the teaching job, her mother and father, who had retired from medical practice, purchased a large, comfortable home in Hays, and Jane decided to give up her small apartment and reside with her parents. She finished her brief biography with the statement that she might soon move out of her parents' home again, as she had become engaged to Max Winn, the state patrolman who had rescued her last winter.

It seems that, besides the physical attraction (Jane, with shoulder-length ash-blonde hair, was about five feet three with her 130 pounds well proportioned), Max had been captivated by her bravery in the life-threatening blizzard and her positive outlook on life in general. During the next hour, while Bob and I ate and drank in silence, except for a few questions for clarity, we were privileged to hear a firsthand account of what has to be one of the most thrilling stories in the annals of rehabilitation teaching of the blind.

Jane usually spent Monday in her office working with her secretary, Sissy Maynard, on progress reports and referrals of her students, answering letters, and planning lessons for the week. Tuesday through Thursday were usually for scheduling long teaching expeditions into outlying counties, with Friday reserved for students in the Hays area. The long teaching excursions often involved three days of travel and two nights in motels for Jane and her driver, Peggy Matthews, a middle-aged housewife who doubled as an Avon distributor and chauffeur. It was one of these trips into the counties northwest of Hays in late January that became a waking nightmare for Peggy and Jane.

When Jane came down to breakfast that Tuesday morning, she heard the crackle of her father's newspaper being folded even before she smelled his cigarette. As she sat down at her usual place to the left of him, he tossed the paper on the buffet behind him and advised, "Better eat a good breakfast, Toots; you and Peg may have to push that old jalopy out of a snowdrift before dinner. Says here that a hell of a snowstorm is pushing southeast across Nebraska and Kansas, winds up to fifty miles per hour piling snow into drifts six feet high in places. I strongly recommend that you take the advice of your family doctor and cancel this fool trip until the weather moderates. None of those blind folks expects you to risk your life to give them a Braille lesson."

"When you first practiced medicine in North Dakota before going to the Army, did you cancel your rural visits every time it snowed?" Jane teased, knowing the response that would erupt from her father.

"Damn it to hell, Janey, you know the circumstances were different. Those folks were sick, some even critical!"

"Just teasing, Dad," Jane laughed. "I just heard a revised weather report from Kansas City. The front is stalled in Nebraska and won't move into Kansas until late tonight or tomorrow. Peggy and I plan to make calls right in Plainville and Stockton and hole up in the Long Horn Motel tonight and just wait out the storm tomorrow if it is too bad to drive on country roads. If necessary, we can extend our trip to three days and work up around Lenora on Thursday. I'll just call Sissy from the motel and have her reschedule my Thursday trip down south toward Lawrence." After further assurance that she would not leave paved highways until the storm passed, her father snapped his paper open to the sports page and continued his breakfast.

When Peggy pulled up in her four-wheel drive Scout instead of her Buick sedan, Jane's father muttered, "There's a smart dame, prepared for the weather." Assuring him that Peggy was a native who knew and respected the changeable weather, Jane ran down the front steps with her briefcase and suitcase in her left hand and her cane and purse in her right hand. As the car pulled into traffic, Jane was telling Peggy about her father's comments on Peggy's shrewdness in dealing with local weather conditions when she noticed they were heading west on Highway 70 rather than north on 183 toward Plainville and Stockton.

"Why are we going west?" Jane inquired.

"You said I was smart about the weather," Peggy replied. "After looking at that itinerary Sissy handed me yesterday and studying several weather bulletins from Kansas City, I've decided to switch today and tomorrow, if it's all right with you. You see," she continued, "that is a real blizzard moving in tonight, and it may drop up to a foot of snow. With the fifty-mile-per-hour winds being forecasted, the roads around Prairie Dog may be impassable for a week, and I heard you say you just had to see that Mr. Wohlwend who lives by himself on that godforsaken ranch east of Prairie Dog."

Jane thought for a moment and asked, "Do you really think we can get in and out of Jess Wohlwend's place before the blizzard hits with full force?" She was compelled to see the widower who had considered suicide after losing his wife to cancer and his vision to glaucoma within the past year. He was just beginning to think life might be worth living, but she feared that lack of contact with anyone but the mailman might cause him to sink back into depression. If she could spend an hour or two providing another cooking lesson and helping Jess reflect on the positive adjustments made by other blind persons whose autobiographies he was reading on talking books, perhaps he would keep up his courage until spring when other ranching activities would occupy his thoughts and he would benefit from social contact with his seasonal employees and neighbors.

While Jane was thinking, Peggy explained that they could make a quick stop in Keeney to deliver the large-print cookbook Jane had ordered for Mrs. Atherton, who still had enough vision to travel without a cane and mow her lawn. Skipping lunch, they could speed north up Highway 183 to the turnoff leading the five miles to Mr. Wohlwend's ranch house, arriving about 1:30 P.M. If they could leave by 3:30, they would be back to Lenora on Highway 183 by dark. If there were no rooms available at the motel, they could stay with Peggy's sister, who had plenty of sleeping accommodations since her children had married and moved away.

As Peggy pulled into Mrs. Atherton's driveway, Jane said she would complete the lesson as soon as possible. After reviewing the format of the large-print cookbook, Jane left Mrs. Atherton trying a new recipe for apple dumplings as she closed the front door and walked rapidly toward the sound of the Scout's idling motor.

Peggy switched on the windshield wiper as they turned onto Highway 183. "I take it that the snow has arrived," Jane observed tentatively.

"Just a few flakes," Peggy answered, "but I think we better go straight to Mr. Wohlwend's so we will be sure to get back to Lenora before the drifts become too deep. The wind is already picking up a little." Their only stop was to fill the twenty-gallon gas tank at a self-service station just north of Keeney. Peggy brought two steaming cups of coffee when she returned from paying for the gasoline, and they enjoyed a snack of coffee and doughnuts while proceeding north on Highway 183 toward Prairie Dog at a steady sixty-five miles per hour. The doughnuts were so tasty that the travelers decided to skip the oranges, potato chips, and Hershey bars that Peggy had also purchased. Peggy tuned in to a nearby radio station, and they listened to Paul Harvey while waiting for a current weather report. The snowstorm was beginning to push slowly into central Kansas, according to the forecaster.

About 2:15 P.M., after driving through the wind-blown snow that cut visibility and collected on the windshield faster than the wipers could remove it, Peggy parked the Scout in front of the Wohlwend ranch house. Jess Wohlwend expressed surprise and concern as he heated a pot of coffee and inquired about the condition of the road between his ranch and the highway. He had figured they would cancel this month's visit, which was scheduled for the following day, when he guessed there would be at least fifteen inches of snow on the ground. When Peggy reported on the road condition and the heavy rate of snowfall, Jess suggested that they either start back to Lenora immediately or plan to stay out the storm at his place. Peggy was sure they could make the return trip safely if they could start back within an hour. Settling herself in Jess's living room with a crossword puzzle, she urged Jane to get on with her lesson so they could leave as soon as possible.

Jane and Jess moved into the kitchen where she proceeded to teach him to attach tiny plastic replicas of beans, ears of corn, and other fruits and vegetables to cans of food so he could identify these items by touch. They also spent time discussing an autobiography of an English gentleman entitled *Whereas I Was Blind*. Peggy terminated this counseling session, in which Jane was using a technique known as bibliotherapy to facilitate Jess's adjustment to his disability, by announcing from the living room that they had to leave now if they were going at all.

Again, Jess recommended they stay at his place until the storm passed. When the women assured him they could make it back to Lenora, Jess placed in the back of their car a five-gallon can of gas drawn from the storage tank used to fuel his farm equipment. "If you get stuck, at least you'll have extra gas to keep the heater going," Jess told them as he closed the car door and made his way the few feet through the swirling snow to his front porch.

Peggy noticed by the sluggish way the Scout handled that the snow was much deeper than it had been an hour ago. For an instant, she considered taking Jess Wohlwend, that kindhearted old German, up on his invitation to remain at his ranch until the storm abated, but the prospect of being isolated away from her family for an indefinite time and her confidence in the ability of her vehicle to plow through the drifts caused her to forge ahead.

With the Scout in four-wheel drive, they made slow but steady progress until the right rear wheel skidded into a deep rut as Peggy was making a sharp left turn at the bottom of a hill; the Scout then came to a sudden stop. Peggy shifted into reverse and tried to ease the Scout backward onto the center of the road, but the wheels spun in place. Finally, Jane suggested that she would try pushing the car from behind in hopes that her added force would be enough for the wheels to catch and pull the vehicle back into the center of the road. Although Jane was physically fit and she threw her entire strength into the forward thrust of the Scout's churning wheels, nothing moved. Jane felt her way back along the right side of the Scout until she located the front door handle. She hopped into the passenger's seat, quickly closing the door to keep out the stinging snow, which was now mixed with sleet.

Peggy retrieved the shovel that she stored in the back of the car for this type of emergency and removed some of the snow in front of each wheel. With Jane pushing again, she tried inching the Scout forward. The front wheels seemed to be catching because the Scout's front end began rocking slightly as first the right and then the left front wheel gained traction. After about a minute, Peggy let the motor idle, and Jane reentered the car. "I'm sorry I got you into this," Peggy said through angry tears, "but if we keep our heads and work together, we can wait here until somebody comes to help."

"That shouldn't take too long," Jane said hopefully. "When we don't arrive for dinner at your sister's in Lenora, she will call Jess Wohlwend, and he will arrange for the state police to rescue us. We shouldn't be stuck here for more than a few hours, even in this blizzard."

Instead of reflecting Jane's optimism, Peggy began crying out loud and said, "I've screwed up things more than you know, Jane. Not only did I change our schedule, but I didn't even tell my sister we were coming. As far as anyone knows, we should be in Stockton, down on Highway 183. We may be here for days. That's why I said we have to work together. We can't make any mistakes, and we have to ration everything so we can make it until help comes."

Suddenly Jane began to feel like the car was closing in on her. She had an illogical compulsion to leap from the vehicle and run to safety, but there was no place to run except into the snowstorm snarling just beyond her car door. She realized that Peggy's loss of control of their situation was causing her friend to panic, and Jane took several deep breaths in order to calm herself before responding to Peggy's distressing analysis of their prospects for survival. She intuitively understood that she must behave calmly and rationally in order to reassure Peggy, whose past experience, judgment, and eyesight were vital to their survival.

"Okay," Jane said with as much bravado as she could muster, "so we're in a little trouble! Let's figure out how to stay warm and entertain ourselves until the posse arrives to rescue us." Jane's show of confidence must have had a settling effect, because Peggy's voice conveyed no sign of tears or despair when she spoke.

"First things first! To keep from freezing—we can't expect to stay warm—we will have to run the motor about fifteen minutes out of every hour. This means that under no circumstances can we both sleep at once because one of us must start the motor every hour, or the engine may get too cold to turn over, and we might quietly snooze ourselves into icebergs."

They decided to alternate sleep periods through the night and try to stay awake during the day in order to respond quickly to any rescue efforts. Peggy estimated that there was at least sixteen gallons of gas in the tank. If they ran the motor at about forty miles per hour, which they could gauge by sound, they should be able to stay fairly warm for about thirty-two hours. At twenty miles per gallon, she calculated they would consume two gallons every hour with the motor turning at forty MPH. This would give them about eight hours of motor operation. By running the motor fifteen minutes every hour, they could make it through the next day and most of the following night, maybe longer if the wind died down and the sun came out to warm the car during the day.

Turning their attention to assuring that their food lasted as long as their gasoline, they gathered all their eatables on the front seat: two Hershey bars, six doughnuts, two oranges, and a small bag of potato chips. "It will be best to save the wrapped stuff and begin with the doughnuts, which will get dried out now that we have opened them," Jane observed, reaching for one.

"You're right," Peggy replied, flicking on the dome light to look at her watch. "It's 5:04 P.M. If we each have a doughnut now, another in the morning, and one each about noon tomorrow, we will not have to start on the packaged stuff until nine tomorrow evening. By splitting the oranges and Hershey bars and rationing ourselves to a half of a Hershey or orange and a few chips for each meal, we will have four more meals that will take us through tomorrow night." The inside of the car was silent for several seconds except for the wind and snow beating against Jane's door.

Finally Peggy continued, "I hate to even think this, let alone say it, but if help doesn't arrive by day after tomorrow, we won't need it."

"Let's cross that bridge when we get there," Jane said with just the hint of a tremor in her voice. "For now, let's think of how we can keep occupied for the next couple of days." Peggy suggested that they listen to the car radio when the motor was running so the battery would remained charged; they might need the lights and continued access to radio information even after the gasoline was all used. Jane remembered that she had her tape player and a recorded book she was returning to the library for Jess Wohlwend. The battery in the tape player would last about ten hours.

So they began their long vigil with Jane taking the first four-hour watch. While Peggy slept, Jane occupied herself by reviewing her life in minute detail, beginning with her first memories of playing with her toy terrier, Tiny, at about age three. She also started the car motor and listened to the radio fifteen minutes every hour, keeping the volume low in order not to disturb Peggy.

As Peggy slept, the sound of wind blowing kept entering her dreams. Most of the time, the wind was woven into dreams of Kansas summers filled with the sounds and visions of wheat and corn being rustled by the warm prairie winds, but once she dreamed of being in a tornado in which her house was severely shaken. When she awoke, the wind was blowing and Jane was shaking her.

"Peggy, I'm sorry to wake you, but it's time for your watch, and, besides, I have to get out of the car to go to the bathroom." Peggy asked Jane to slide out the driver's side, as this would leave the wall of snow that had blown against Jane's side of the vehicle intact, forming a windbreak. Returning to the warm car, which Peggy had started, Jane had no trouble drifting into a sound sleep. Her dreams centered around the early childhood memories she had been recalling. Just before she woke up, she saw herself in the midst of a winter afternoon playing with her toy terrier in the snow, but everything turned unpleasant when the dog became lost in a snowdrift and her father appeared to berate her for her poor judgment in taking the little animal out in such deep snow. When Peggy aroused her for the 2:00 A.M. watch, she was cold and wanted something to eat, but Peggy reminded her that it would be a long time until lunch if she ate breakfast at two in the morning. She settled for a handful of snow and began listening to the radio for any mention of their being lost in the blizzard.

When Peggy roused about six, her first words were, "Have you heard anything about a search party yet?" Jane hadn't heard a thing about anyone being lost, but she immediately switched on the radio to a local station that carried "The Sunrise News" and, within five minutes, heard an item about two women from Hays who had been missing for about twenty-four hours. The announcer explained that they had not been seen since leaving Hays yesterday for the Stockton area, where they were scheduled to conduct state business. The item was clustered with many emergency announcements such as school closings, electrical power failures, and highway closures, including Highway 183 north of Lenora, which was impassable due to drifting snow.

"Looks like no rescue party will be coming up 183 today," Peggy observed.

After their breakfast of doughnuts and melted snow, they spent an hour listening to the recorded book, diligently devoting fifteen minutes each hour to warm up the car and turn on the radio. They followed the same schedule through the afternoon and evening, with two or three hours out for naps and conversation. The wind died down about noon, and the sun came out about 2:30, warming the inside of the car and conserving about a gallon of gas. The 3:00 P.M. news carried the announcement that an air search was being conducted within a fifty-mile radius of Stockton, which was very discouraging to Peggy and Jane; they were probably beyond the perimeter of the search area. Once they heard an aircraft fly over at a high altitude. Scurrying from the Scout, they waved a dark blanket that they had been using for warmth, but the pilot made no maneuver of recognition.

With only three meals left after their dinner of a half of an orange and a few chips each, they talked for a long time about their prospects and what they could do to improve them. Looking out her window at the glare of the moon on the miles of snow in all directions, Peggy suddenly said, "That moon will be down about midnight, and I have an idea for attracting some attention. Most people may be asleep, but all we need is for one person to investigate the fire."

"What the hell are you talking about?" laughed Jane. "Are you planning to burn the car?"

"Not exactly," Peggy said. "I forgot to tell you that there is a haystack about fifty feet outside my window. You remember that five-gallon can of gas Jess put in the back of the Scout? Well, I figure we can take the shovel and tunnel into the dry hay and set it afire with about a half a gallon of gas to get it started. It will be visible for miles on such a clear night, and somebody is bound to get curious and investigate." So, they each worked ten-minute shifts until they burrowed far enough into the haystack to reach dry hay, after which they excavated a small hole up through the hay until the shovel broke through into the moonlight. This hole would serve as a chimney for the fireplace. Jane worried about the sparks, but Peggy assured her that there was enough snow on the car to extinguish any sparks.

Peggy saturated the dry hay with gasoline and wove some straws into a long strip so she could use them to light the hay from a distance of several feet. Jane waited in the car with Peggy's door open so she could quickly retreat to safety if the haystack exploded. This precaution proved unnecessary, however, because the fire spread slowly at first, allowing Peggy ample time to retreat behind the closed car door, where she was able to observe the flame progress slowly into the tunnel they had dug until it reached the small vertical shaft; then the haystack erupted, pelting the car with a mixture of snow and sparks. Both women ducked reflexively, but Peggy had been right in assuming that the layer of snow would extinguish any burning hay that reached the car. Within a few seconds, the exploding haystack had settled into a bright mound of flame that could be seen for several miles.

As the minutes grew into hours and no rancher appeared to determine who had destroyed his valuable supply of cattle feed, the women resumed their former routine, discouraged by the realization that their salvation would not depend on help from others but on their own ingenuity and efforts. After the fire died, Peggy somberly poured the remaining gasoline into the Scout's tank so they could stay relatively warm for another day, and they shared the last orange and the remaining chips for breakfast just after sunrise.

As Peggy switched off the 10:00 A.M. news, which reported that the search for the missing female state employees was continuing around Stockton, she placed her right arm around Jane's shoulders and said, "Listen, kid, we can't just sit here and wait for the end without trying. There probably is enough gas in the tank to keep the car warm until tomorrow, if you depend on the heat of the sun through the day." Jane began to feel like her stomach and heart were contracting and knew she was experiencing panic because Peggy was telling her that she would have to stay alone while Peggy went for help. And what if she didn't find any?

Peggy was saying, "By using the sun for direction, I can walk due west and strike the highway, which can't be more than a mile. Then I can head south toward Lenora for help. I hate to leave you here alone, not only because you may feel trapped in the car by the snow, but because I'm scared to death to start out across that open white prairie without another person along for encouragement. I have to do it, though, because the two of us would move too slowly to reach help in time."

Jane had to exert all of her self-control to keep from physically restraining Peggy as she stuffed one of the two remaining Hershey bars into her coat, kissed Jane reassuringly on the cheek, and closed the car door behind her. Ignoring the loss of precious heat stored inside the vehicle, Jane rolled down her window and listened to the sound of Peggy's boots until her steps disappeared into the silence of the Kansas landscape. Since there was no chilling wind, the sun quickly reheated the interior when the window had been closed, but Jane couldn't stand the isolation and again lowered the window to listen for the sound of a bird or any other living thing. When she began to shiver from the cold, she again rolled up the window and switched on the radio. Human voices, even disembodied voices with whom she could establish no contact, might be able to distract and calm her temporarily. Jane pulled the blanket tightly around her, which seemed to reduce her feeling of solitude slightly, and tuned the radio to a classical music broadcast. Finally, the soft music and the warmth of the sun shining on her blanket relaxed Jane, and she drifted into a comfortable sleep.

After what seemed an indefinite period of time during which she was floating in a warm and secure environment, Jane became conscious of a hand on her wrist and a kind male voice. "Jane, can you hear me?" it asked. In sleepy confusion, she assumed the voice belonged to the radio announcer, and the feelings of isolation and despair overwhelmed her. When she began to cry and burrow further into her blanket, her wrist was released, and a comforting, strong arm enfolded her. It suddenly occurred to Jane that radio voices did not hug people.

The voice resumed, "You're safe, Jane. I'm Max Winn, a highway patrolman, and I'm going to take care of you." Max explained that he had found Peggy walking on Highway 183 as he was driving his Jeep north from Lenora to determine if the road could safely be reopened. She was waiting in the warm Jeep for Max to walk to the Scout and rescue Jane, as not even a Jeep could traverse the back roads.

Jane could not wait to get out of the car and start for Max's Jeep. They trudged through knee-deep snow for about a half mile before ascending a short but steep hill, and Peggy's cheery voice welcomed them back into the vehicle. It took about thirty minutes to get back to Peggy's sister's house in Lenora, where she had hot food and a bath waiting for them, having been contacted by phone from state police headquarters following Max's radio report.

Bob and I relaxed as Jane finished her story with an account of how Max had continued to visit her, ostensibly to fill in necessary information on his rescue report, finally asking her for a date. One date led to another, and now they had set a wedding date. According to Jane, the wedding was developing into a media extravaganza because of the extensive press coverage following her survival and rescue from the blizzard. She had even received a proclamation from the governor recognizing her devotion to duty under adverse conditions along with a resolution from the state legislature praising her bravery and commending Max for heroism in rescuing her from a life-threatening situation.

As I took leave of Jane and Bob at the entrance to the hotel dining room, I suggested to Jane that her story could be made into a hit movie, and, after preparing this sketch at least fifteen years since hearing her narration, my opinion has not changed.

PART TWO

LEARNING TO WORK WITH BLINDNESS: VOCATIONAL COUNSELING

The oldest historical documents relating to blind people describe efforts to place them in jobs that could be performed without eyesight. An ancient Chinese ruler decreed that the occupations of soothsayer and masseur would be reserved exclusively for blind persons, and special schools were established to prepare them for these trades. In ancient Rome, blind boys were employed as oarsmen. Around 1800, the French government established a program to incorporate blind people into their society by separating them according to five levels of economic functioning: those who engaged in business and professions such as law, music, or teaching; those who performed skilled crafts, such as piano tuning; those who engaged in home industry; those who worked and lived in sheltered workshops attached to communal living facilities; and those blind persons who, because of additional disabilities or age, were unable to do any significant work and were housed in what we might term group homes today. When we remember that Emperor Napoleon was involved in the greatest military expansion in European history, it seems remarkable that the French government would have had the compassion or resources to engage in such an elaborate employment program for a relatively small group of its disabled citizens. However, this relationship between militarism and the expansion of employment opportunities for the blind has continued down to the present century.

Due to the sedentary and repetitive nature of assembly-line work, leaders in work for the blind recognized the opportunities for their clients in manufacturing in the early part of the twentieth century. During World War I, for example, the Crocker Wheeler Company, a manufacturing firm in Newark, New Jersey, employed one hundred blind workers in a special unit that inspected and packed finished products. Following World War II, the Radio Corporation of America established the practice of employing one blind worker for every thousand sighted workers.

Because the public had little understanding or tolerance of disabled people in the early twentieth century, it is difficult to understand how workers for the blind were able to persuade employers to permit blind persons to tour their factories, let alone actually allow them to operate machinery. This seemingly impossible task of securing industrial employment for blind persons was accomplished largely through the direct demonstration of capable placement agents who were blind themselves, such as Joe Klunk. Klunk was so successful in talking his way into factories, where he would demonstrate the performance of selected jobs without sight, that he became the first director of the U.S. Office of Vocational Rehabilitation for the Blind. With the establishment of college training programs in rehabilitation counseling, it was possible to combine the academic knowledge of college-trained counselors with the job placement skills devised by such pioneers as Joe Klunk to provide agencies for the blind with placement counselors who could address the psychological problems of adjusting to blindness and confront the practical problems of securing employment for blind persons.

The stories in this chapter were selected, in part, because they focus on the personal characteristics of fierce independence, mental and manual competency, and personal integrity demonstrated by successful vocational counselors of the blind, such as Joe Klunk, J. D. McCawley, and George Magers. A central character in these narratives is Bob Wright, who graduated from the Illinois School for the Visually Impaired, earned a master's degree in rehabilitation from the University of Illinois, and completed the training course in job placement of the blind conducted by Louis Vieceli at Southern Illinois University. Both in his personal life and thirty-three-year career as a vocational counselor for the blind, Bob demonstrated outstanding ability to do manual work and deal with complicated concepts of economics, industrial relations, and rehabilitation. He was at ease in a graduate seminar, working on plumbing and other home repairs, or cutting firewood with his chain saw. Particularly in "The Wrong Wright," Bob's behavior reveals the independence, resourcefulness, and adventurous spirit that are the foundational characteristics of a successful vocational rehabilitation counselor of blind persons.

8

THE WRONG WRIGHT

On the Fourth of July, 1971, I was contemplating the Declaration of Independence when the phone interrupted my reverie. "Do you know what day this is?" demanded a gruff voice. It was Bob Wright, my closest friend and professional colleague in the field of blind rehabilitation, inviting me to join him at the American Legion later that day for a few drinks in celebration of the Fourth. Accordingly, I notified my wife that some urgent business required my attention and headed for the Legion.

The odor of cigarette smoke and stale beer greeted me. "Your buddy is already here," Pete, the bartender, told me. Bob was seated on a stool about midway down the bar, flanked on his right by Bob Dickerson. I took the stool on the other side and accepted the can of Pabst that Bob had ordered when he heard my heel cleats coming through the door. Both Bob and I had begun wearing metal cleats when we were students at the Illinois School for the Blind in the late 1940s to enhance auditory detection of objects; the echoes created by the sound of the cleats bounced off cars, posts, and the like.

Bill Cargill mounted the stool to my left and began telling how a kid tossed a lighted cherry bomb under his truck, almost causing a wreck. Setting a beer before Bill to settle his nerves,

Pete remarked that it was fortunate that Bill had encountered the cherry bomb on the way to the Legion, as he would have been in poor shape for avoiding a wreck after a couple of six-packs. Bill's incident with the cherry bomb prompted others at the bar to recall past experiences with fireworks. One patron told how he and some other boys had once arranged a race between two tomcats with firecrackers tied to their tails, wagering on which cat could run faster when the firecrackers exploded. Someone told of a friend who had lost his sight when a firecracker exploded in his face, and B. J. told of a teenager setting off a cherry bomb in the restroom of a bus he was driving. Bob Wright said he would tell a firecracker story if I would buy a round. When Pete had served the drinks, Bob began his tale.

Bob explained that he had always been fascinated by firecrackers and other things that made loud noises. For example, he told of sitting under a railway bridge near the School for the Blind when he was about ten years old in order to experience the excitement of the rumbling noise created by the trains passing overhead. As Bob grew into an adult, he adopted the practice of celebrating the Fourth of July with plenty of fireworks.

In 1951, Bob had been making plans to celebrate the Fourth of July with Tooney Jordon since the beginning of the spring quarter at Southern Illinois University. Bob and Tooney, his friend and former schoolmate at the Illinois School for the Blind, had celebrated the 1950 Fourth, along with several other friends from Bob's work, with as much vigor and enjoyment as a keg of beer and twenty-five dollars worth of assorted firecrackers could provide. Bob phoned Tooney in early May of 1951 to let him know that this year's Independence Day would be even more exciting because Bob would arrive at Tooney's place in Chicago the day before the Fourth with a suitcase filled with fireworks.

On the night of July 2, Bob packed his Samsonite suitcase with a shaving kit and two changes of clothes wrapped around as many firecrackers, cherry bombs, Roman candles, and other assorted fireworks as he could stuff into the remaining space. Early on the morning of the third, he hefted the heavy case and walked the four blocks from his room over the University Drug Store to John's Cafe, where he used fifty cents of his five-dollar meal ticket to eat a hearty breakfast before setting off on his hitchhiking trip to visit Tooney. When Irene, John's wife, punched the meal ticket, she remarked that Bob must be leaving for an extended vacation, judging from the size of his suitcase. Bob assured her that he would be back in town in a week and headed north to Main Street where he could catch his first ride.

Stationing himself under a large tree, Bob began holding up his right hand with the thumb extended each time he heard the motor of an oncoming vehicle. Luck was with him, because the fourth car glided to a stop and a not-unfriendly voice said, "You've got a ride, son. Get in!"

After traveling a few miles, the car slowed noticeably and pulled into a parking space.

"Where are we?" Bob asked.

The voice from the driver's seat quipped, "Being from Indiana, I know you're a little backward, but I can't believe you never seen a police station before."

"If you're going to be here long, I'll just walk back to the highway and catch another ride because I'm kind of in a hurry," Bob informed his companion.

"Not until we have a little talk! So you just quietly get out and follow me into my office without any fuss," drawled the driver.

"Who are you, anyway?" Bob asked, a note of belligerence in his voice.

"This badge you see on my coat says I'm the sheriff of Jackson County," the voice said, while hustling Bob into the south entrance of the Jackson County Courthouse. Just inside the first door on the right of the hall leading to the rotunda, Bob tripped on a chair but quickly regained his balance.

"Little shaky on your feet, are you? Here is a cup of coffee to settle your nerves. Just relax in that chair you kicked and read this wire from the White County sheriff and tell me where you left the car you borrowed from that grocery store operator in Carmi," ordered the sheriff.

"Oh shit!" thought Bob. "He's got me mixed up with somebody else, and he thinks I can see." Taking a large swallow of the hot coffee, Bob said, in what he hoped was a confident and rational voice, "Sheriff, this little confusion is easy to straighten out. You think I'm some guy who stole a car, but, you see, my name is Wright, and I'm a student at SIU."

"According to that telegram you're holding, you are half right. Your name is Wright McGee, but your most recent address was the White County jail. After you walked away from a work detail, you robbed the Red and White Grocery in Crossville, took the owner's 1947 Ford sedan, which you ditched somewhere, and were trying to thumb your way to St. Louis or Chicago when I conveniently noticed that you pretty well fit the description from the White County sheriff." The sheriff removed the paper from Bob's hand, and his now-familiar voice read: "'Five feet five inches tall; about 140 pounds; very muscular; brown eyes and hair.' A pretty accurate description, wouldn't you say?"

Bob cleared his voice and replied. "I'll admit, it looks like I'm your suspect from that description, but there is one fact you are forgetting that makes it impossible for me to be the guy who stole the car. A blind person can't drive."

The sheriff pitched the telegram on his desk, leaned back in his creaking, swiveling chair, and observed Bob for several seconds before speaking. "You're reachin' pretty far out for an alibi, Wright. You are looking straight at me, you didn't have any trouble getting into my car or walking in here, except when your foot caught on that chair leg because being so near to another county jail made you a little nervous, and no blind man walks on a highway without a dog or cane. Besides, you answered to the name of Wright," the sheriff stated, finalizing his reasoning.

Bob wondered where to go from here with his attempt to convince the sheriff he had made a mistake. Should he tell the lawman that he had a cane folded in his suitcase? No way! This would get him arrested for illegal transportation of fireworks. He would have to convince the sheriff that he had forgotten to pack his cane, though Bob had a feeling that this explanation would not satisfy his interrogator. Well, it was the best thing he could think of at the moment.

Bob finished his coffee and began. "As to my seeming to know my own name, my name is Robert Wright. You just called me Wright, which I'm used to because a lot of my teachers and friends call me that. I can't explain why the guy you are confusing me with has the same first name as my last name. Maybe you could ask his mother. The reason I'm not carrying a cane is because I like to see if I can get around without one. Besides, I would have had one if I hadn't left it in my room over the University Drug Store." When Bob finished, there was another long silence.

Finally, the sheriff informed Bob that he would make inquiries in Carbondale, and if Bob's story checked out, he could be on his way to wherever it was he was going.

"How long will this take?" Bob asked.

The sheriff responded, "A few hours."

It was already 8:30 in the morning, and Bob could imagine arriving at Tooney's after the Fourth was over. He played his last card.

"Look," Bob said in what he hoped was a concerned voice, "I know you are very busy checking on such crimes as illegal sales of fireworks"—a bad example—"so I have a way to save you the time of going to Carbondale and talking with people who can vouch for me. I'm sure you know where John's Cafe is on South Illinois Street in Carbondale. I just had breakfast there about an hour ago. You can just phone John or his wife, Irene, and either will tell you where I live and that I eat there every day except Sunday on a meal ticket."

This course of action seemed to appeal to the sheriff because he began turning pages of what Bob figured was a phone book, after which he spoke the phone number of John's Cafe to the operator. Bob could hear Irene's raised voice from the phone across the room after the sheriff informed her of his detention and what the charge was. When the sheriff asked if Bob had eaten there that morning and if he had a cane, Irene's voice again filled the phone for several seconds. Her explanation must have been satisfactory because the sheriff said, "He goes all over town by himself without a cane?"

Hanging up the phone, the sheriff's now very friendly voice said, "Mr. Wright, I owe you an apology. Miss Irene assures me that you are, indeed, a regular customer, an outstanding student at SIU, and a close friend of Mayor Wright of Carbondale." He offered to make amends for his error in confusing Bob with Wright McGee by taking him back to his room and helping him pack his cane in his bag. Not wanting the sheriff within a mile when the suitcase filled with fireworks was opened, Bob convinced him that he could pick up another cane when he stopped to visit his parents in Shelbyville. The sheriff finally felt he had been helpful enough when he took Bob to a truck stop and put him in contact with a truck driver who gave him a ride all the way to Pana, Illinois.

After arriving at Tooney's place about 2:00 A.M. on the Fourth of July, Bob slept in until about noon, but everyone at that Independence Day celebration reported that Bob's fireworks made the party more fun than the 1950 blowout.

9

THE WET CONVERTIBLE

The rhythmic tap of shoe cleats stopped in front of the ticket window, alerting Herb, the ticket agent of the Peoria Rockford Bus Company, that a potential customer had arrived. Completing the entry in his tariff log, he peered over the top of his reading glasses at Bob Wright, a regular rider who used the bus several times a month for traveling to communities in southern Illinois to perform his job of rehabilitation counselor for the blind. Today, he was embarking on a two-day trip to Harrisburg, where he could join up with another counselor, Harker Miley, for the purpose of calling on joint clients and potential employers for these clients. Bob scooped up his round-trip ticket and the twenty-five cents change from his five-dollar bill. "Have these damn bus tickets gone up again?" he asked.

"This is the 1960s," replied the agent. "When you state workers get a raise, my taxes go up, and I pass the increase on to my bus riders," Herb joked. "According to the *Southern Illusion*"—Herb's nickname for the *Southern Illinoisan* newspaper—"Governor Kerner has promised you boys a big raise, so we went ahead and raised the tickets in order to get the jump on you."

"Since you're raising my bus fare even before I get a raise, I guess you're providing additional services like storing my bag until bus time free of charge," rejoined Bob.

Herb stepped from behind the counter and took Bob's suitcase ceremoniously, stating that it would be an honor to look after the luggage of an important state employee. With an appropriate response, Bob left the bus station and crossed the street to Sobery's Bakery, where he bought a dozen doughnuts, after which he walked a block north to the Carbondale office of the Department of Public Welfare.

Like the bus agent, I heard the sound of Bob's heel cleats coming down the hall. Stepping into my small office, he announced, "Mr. Roberts! This is an official call to discuss joint cases, but I don't suppose you would mind eating a couple of doughnuts while we talk." Leaving Bob to arrange his papers, I went across the alley to Walgreen's Drugstore for two cups of coffee, after which we got down to business.

Since the Harrisburg bus would not leave for another hour, we had time for a brief review of the joint cases Bob would be working on during the next two days. Sally Meyer, age twenty, was a high school graduate in need of concentrated training in Braille, cane travel, typing, and other basic skills of independent living that would necessitate her spending four months at the Illinois Visually Handicapped Institute in Chicago. A small-town girl with close family ties, Sally was presenting one reason after another why she could not go to Chicago. Because Bob was certain that she would not succeed in the job market without these basic skills, we spent some time brainstorming strategies that would convince Sally to at least begin the training program. Sally felt she must have help from the Division of Vocational Rehabilitation in order to achieve her goal of becoming a secretary, so it was finally decided that Bob would present her with the options of either proceeding with the necessary training or else changing her objective to some unskilled job that required minimal training at home. I would make a follow-up visit in a couple of weeks to offer support and understanding of her reluctance to leave the security of her home along with such incentives as an escort for the train trip to

Chicago. Two other cases requiring joint planning were reviewed so that Bob could begin to implement changes in approach during his two-day itinerary with Harker Miley, who worked out of the Harrisburg DVR office.

In those days, vocational counselors for the blind provided technical consultation on blindness and job placement services to general counselors, like Mr. Miley, who actually managed all rehabilitation cases, including the blind, deaf, orthopedically disabled, and other categories. Therefore, Bob and Harker would plan two or three days every month for joint contacts, with Harker providing the transportation because, as Harker explained, "I'm a better driver than Bob."

Exactly five minutes before departure time for the Harrisburg bus, Bob replaced his Braille slate and conference notes in his briefcase and rushed across the street to the bus station. My thoughts did not return to Bob until about 5:30 Friday afternoon when we met at the American Legion to rehash the week's work and unwind with a few beers. Tom North, the business enterprise counselor for the disabled in southern Illinois, and Bob were already settled at a table near the bowling machine when I came in.

Tom asked, "What's the latest adventure of Counselor Miley? Is he engaged in any new business venture or other exciting activity?"

"The most exciting thing in Harker's life this week is his new convertible, a shiny red Pontiac with leather seats. We just spent a day and a half taking this red beauty on a maiden voyage around Saline, Galatin, and Massac Counties," Bob answered, finishing his first can of Pabst.

"Knowing you and Harker, I suppose you christened this new chariot with a little Jack Daniels," Tom hypothesized.

"You're pretty close to what happened," Bob said, beginning his story.

After leaving my office to board the Harrisburg bus, Bob took his bag from the ticket agent, who said a Mr. Miley had phoned to say that he would meet Bob at the Harrisburg bus station with a surprise. Based on past experience with Harker Miley,

Bob spent some time during the hour-long ride trying to imagine what practical joke would be awaiting him when the bus pulled into the station.

"Be careful; that last step is a high one," said the driver, grasping Bob's left elbow as he hopped to the pavement with his suitcase in one hand and briefcase in the other.

A familiar voice spoke as Bob's bags were whisked away. "Robert, get off that rusty old bus and come with me. From here on, we're going in style." If he had not known this voice belonged to Harker Miley, Bob might have imagined he was being chauffeured by Clark Gable, for Miley's laugh and voice tone could easily be confused with Rhett Butler's. After an exaggerated performance in which Harker opened the car door for Bob and placed his bags on the back seat, the car was speeding away from the bus station when Bob noticed the wind flowing over the windshield.

"What the hell kind of car is this?" he asked. "Don't tell me, you've borrowed a convertible to impress our clients and employer contacts."

"I told the guy in the Carbondale bus station to tell you to expect a surprise," Miley shouted over the wind as the car turned on Route 45 and accelerated like an airplane taking off. "This is the surprise, a brand-spanking-new Pontiac convertible, red with whitewall tires, AM and FM radio, and genuine leather seats. Bobby," Miley shouted into the wind, "we will be the most popular gallants in Old Shawneetown tonight."

Remarking that they would have to wait until the afternoon calls were completed before they could enjoy the pleasures of Old Shawneetown, Bob settled back to enjoy the full experience of the convertible ride to Eldorado, where their first client resided.

When the convertible pulled into the yard, a young woman of about twenty years and a middle-aged couple were seated in metal lawn chairs under an elm tree next to a one-story frame house with a screened front porch. The young lady had been the subject of the consultation in the public welfare office that morning. Bob and Harker spent an hour talking about the need for the younger woman to attend the Illinois Visually Handicapped Institute in Chicago or else to change her vocational goal to an occupation requiring fewer specialized skills. At last, with the encouragement of her parents, she agreed to attend the institute if she and her family could be sure that the rehabilitation teacher from the Carbondale office would arrange for an escort on her first trip to Chicago and handle some other issues related to the continuance of her public assistance grant.

The second, and last, contact that afternoon was with a blind man who practiced the unusual occupation of diving into rivers and lakes to recover submerged items. This man and his son took turns diving on sunken barges and other submerged vessels with the use of World War II divers' gear. Due to the murkiness of the Ohio River water, the father, who was totally dependent on nonvisual information, could often locate and secure underwater items better than his sighted son. The most publicized project completed by this unusual team was the raising of several dozen new cars that had been dumped into the river when a barge capsized. The reason for this visit was to discuss a request for help in purchasing some new equipment. Although the diving twosome were able to earn enough to meet basic living needs, they could never save enough to update their obsolete diving rig. It was finally decided that the case would be referred to the business enterprise counselor, and Harker headed the convertible south toward Old Shawneetown.

Bob and Harker, their hair rumpled and faces tingling from the wind, spent a pleasant evening visiting the establishments on both sides of the main street in Old Shawneetown. They began with a fiddler catfish dinner at Logston's Tavern, then crossed the street to a bar located in what appeared to be an abandoned store or warehouse. Having no windows except at the street door, the place was illuminated only by a couple of light bulbs extended from the ceiling and the neon signs behind the bar. After an hour in a dance hall, similar to the previous establishment with the exception of a three-piece band and several couples dancing to country music, Bob and Harker drove back to Harrisburg with the convertible top down and the radio blaring. As Bob entered the lobby of the Horning Hotel, he could still hear the music from the convertible radio as Harker turned the corner and headed for his home in Eldorado.

When Bob left the hotel the following morning, a night rain had freshened the air, and the early warmth of the sun seemed to enhance the odor of damp grass flavored with lilacs growing in the yard. He met with Harker at his office in Harrisburg, where they completed a rundown of what needed to be accomplished with their four scheduled clients. Picking up the convertible in the parking lot, they headed for Rosiclaire.

The ride in the open car refreshed and invigorated the passengers, who had been a little sluggish from inadequate sleep the previous night. Turning north off the state highway just east of Rosiclaire, Miley picked his way over a rough gravel road, pulling into a lane that terminated at the top of a steep hill. The rock lane ended about two feet from the kitchen porch of the four-room house where the blind client resided with her husband and six-month-old baby. Since Bob was visiting to review a list of adapted homemaking and child care equipment recommended by the rehabilitation teacher for purchase by the Division of Vocational Rehabilitation, Harker decided to remain in the car to catch up on his paperwork and enjoy the beautiful summer weather.

The young mother appeared in the kitchen door holding her baby and greeted Bob warmly. She was lavish in her appreciation for the help both she and her husband, whom she had met at the Illinois Visually Handicapped Institute, were receiving. The plan for this small family was for the training in homemaking received at the institute to be supplemented with special equipment and training from the local rehabilitation teacher. This equipment and training would enable the new mother to care for her child and house independently, allowing her husband, who retained partial vision and had been doing much of the housework, to become gainfully employed.

Bob spent about thirty minutes discussing exactly how each item of equipment would relieve the husband from household duties. Just as he was replacing his Braille writer in its case, the young woman insisted on bringing him a glass of iced tea from the kitchen. Handing him the glass, she said, "Just enjoy your tea for a minute while I dump my cold dishwater. You know, we haven't got sewage out here yet, but we hope to afford it if John gets a job."

The next sounds Bob heard were the slam of the kitchen screen door, a car motor erupting into action, and tires spinning on gravel. Returning to the living room, the young woman said, "Is there someone waiting for you in a car? I heard a car leave when I went out to dump the dishwater over the back porch railing."

Like Bob, Harker had heard the screen door slam and glanced up from his notebook. When the young woman stepped to the porch rail, he knew that his red convertible was going to be christened with the breakfast dishwater and any food residue floating in it. With one body movement, he shifted into reverse and hit the starter. As the car shot backward, a cloud of greasy brown suds seemed to hang in the air over the hood and windshield, finally settling like a gently falling blanket from the top of the windshield to the foxtail ornament on the grill. Miraculously, the rapid backward movement of the car had saved the leather upholstery. There were only a couple of brown spots on the rearview mirror, which Miley wiped with his handkerchief.

Hearing the car turn around at the foot of the hill and head for the main road, Bob realized that Harker had probably gone to a car wash. Therefore, he passed another half hour in pleasant conversation with the client, inquiring about her family, asking about friendships developed during her training in Chicago, and admiring her baby. At last, the car labored about halfway up the hill and stopped. Bob surmised that Harker was trying to keep out of dishwater-throwing range. Taking leave of the young lady, he used his cane to locate the porch steps and walked down to the parked convertible, which felt as clean as a whistle when he trailed his hand along the right front fender to locate the door.

Turning around toward the main highway, Harker said, "Bobby, your clients are dangerous." He went on to explain his good luck in escaping any water damage inside the convertible. "A fifty-cent car wash, which means you owe me a drink, erased all traces of the grease and scum," he elaborated.

The other calls were completed without any surprises. A visit to a plumber, recently blinded when the chemical he was using to open a clogged sewer exploded, resulted in his decision to investigate guide dog training before choosing a new vocation. Arrangements for a client in her mid-thirties to visit a cafeteria operated by another blind woman was set for the following month. She wanted firsthand information on this type of employment in order to decide if she wanted to enter vending facility training. The last visit before Harker dropped Bob off at the bus station was to check on the success of a man, blind from birth with no formal education, who had recently been provided machinery for manufacturing brooms for sale throughout southern Illinois. Harker and Bob worked with this man on a plan for marketing and distributing his product. Since his lack of basic math and reading skills ruled out the use of Braille for bookkeeping, it was decided that the client would enter sales and other transactions on a tape recorder, which would enable his brother, who lived with him, to maintain a business ledger.

Bob napped during the bus ride to Carbondale and then carried his bags to the Legion where he narrated the story of the wet convertible. "So you see, Tom, your remark about Miley christening his new convertible sized up the situation pretty well."

1 0

BEHIND THE SHAKING DOOR

A mind teaser encountered by most persons who are deaf or blind is, "Which is more limiting, deafness or blindness?" Of course, the answer usually differs according to the disability of the person responding to the question. A deaf person, having learned to depend on vision to perceive information usually acquired through hearing, will most often consider blindness the more limiting condition. Conversely, the blind person, trained to depend on hearing for obtaining information acquired by sighted peers through vision, often believes that deafness is the more limiting disability. Probably the only definitive answer would come from persons who are deprived of both sight and hearing, of whom there are several thousand in the United States. The most well known, of course, was Helen Keller, but there have been many others who have achieved fame in literature, education, rehabilitation, and other professions as well as a much larger group engaged in manufacturing and service occupations.

People who become both deaf and blind are often served by the Blindness Rehabilitation System, and, although few in number, these multiply disabled persons present rehabilitation teachers and counselors with the most complicated challenge to their professional competency. As to the question of whether deafness or blindness is the more limiting disability, professionals disagree, but most do agree that the combination of deafness and blindness creates a handicap much more severe than either would by itself. Persons disabled in this way are denied access to such perceptions as music and painting, differential movement of people and objects through space, ease of communication with others, and the security of visual and auditory warnings in their environments.

Because of the high degree of professional competency required to facilitate the rehabilitation of this small but extremely deserving and important group of multiply disabled persons, those of us involved in the hiring of professional workers for the blind usually focus a segment of each employment interview on the candidate's potential for working with people who are both blind and deaf. This phase of the interview in April 1976 weighed heavily in my selection of Jo Carol Gulley for the position of rehabilitation teacher for the five Illinois counties bordering the Mississippi River south of St. Louis. Besides having a degree in special education and an enthusiastic manner, Jo had performed well in her practice teaching assignment at a school for the deaf. It seemed reasonable that she would be able to acquire a working knowledge of the eleven systems for communicating with deaf-blind persons contained in the small reference manual *Methods of Communication with the Deaf-Blind*, found in the bookcase of every rehabilitation teacher employed by the state of Illinois. Communication with deaf-blind persons differs from signing to deaf people, who perceive signs visually, because of the necessity to form letters and signs in the hand of the deaf-blind person. However, Jo was able to adapt her communication style to the deaf-blind with ease. First as a rehabilitation teacher and more recently as a vocational counselor, she has continued to demonstrate professional competency in providing rehabilitation services to persons who are both blind and deaf.

During one home visit to a deaf-blind college student, Jo became involved in an embarrassing and potentially dangerous situation. She first became acquainted with Jeff Kelley during his sophomore Individual Educational Planning (IEP) conference at the Illinois School for the Visually Impaired in Jacksonville. Each spring, all vocational rehabilitation counselors who had high school students from their local areas in attendance at this school were required to be present at the students' IEP conferences. Jeff's conferences were usually more complicated and time-consuming than those of other students, partly because Jeff was both deaf and legally blind and partly because his vocational goal of becoming an educator involved his going to college. His mental capacity for college was not in question (he consistently scored above 120 on I.Q. tests); but the multitude of arrangements for obtaining special textbooks and equipment, working out convenient housing, locating note-takers for lectures, and preparing Jeff and his family to deal with the many other barriers created by his dual disabilities resulted in long conferences. Although completely deaf, Jeff did retain 20-200 visual acuity, which is the upper limit of legal blindness, and he had learned to read large print and write fluently. During his junior and senior years, he also became proficient in using a personal computer with a monitor that could magnify print.

Having been on the swimming and wrestling teams at the Illinois School for the Visually Impaired, Jeff continued in these sports at Southern Illinois University, along with such other extracurricular activities as attending parties and dating. Probably because of his outgoing personality and willingness to explain the nature of his disabilities to others, he found many able-bodied students willing to invest a little extra time to communicate by printing letters in his palm, writing on a notepad he carried just for this purpose, or learning the one-handed alphabet for the deaf. Jeff consistently made B's and a few A's, and he was generally popular with his professors and other people in the community, including several deaf friends.

During his first year at SIU, Jeff met frequently with Counselor Gulley, but as arrangements for housing, transportation, note-takers, and other necessary supports became routine, the time between counseling sessions lengthened to three or four months. Sometimes he would come into the office to deal with some problem in processing payment for tuition or for other services, but more often Jo would visit at his residence. Because an appointment letter would arrive at his dorm a few days prior to Jo's visit, Jeff was usually expecting her. This pattern continued with no problem until Jeff moved in with a friend who was deaf but had normal eyesight.

The move occurred in the middle of the last semester in Jeff's senior year. Jo was anxious to begin regular counseling sessions in preparation for assisting Jeff in locating and securing a suitable teaching position. The problem was that Jeff had left no forwarding address and, therefore, could not be notified of Jo's intended visit by the usual appointment letter. After several contacts with members of the deaf community, Jo learned that Jeff was sharing a trailer with a friend who was employed at a manufacturing plant and was also deaf. The two young men were located in a trailer court between Carbondale and Herrin. She could not obtain a mailing address, but Jeff's friend was able to describe the location of the trailer in the park because he had attended a party there the last weekend.

On a clear Tuesday morning in early April, Jo drove her Toyota sedan into the trailer park where Jeff Kelley and his friend, Andy Sprague, resided. She stepped out of the car to inquire about the exact location of Jeff's trailer from an elderly man mowing the lawn around a double-wide mobile home with newly planted maple trees and rock-bordered flower beds attractively placed about the yard. The man glanced at Jo's ID card with "Department of Rehabilitation Services" printed across the top. He said DORS was welcome to any assistance he could give, explaining that he was familiar with the department because his granddaughter, who had a speech impairment, was receiving college tuition from this agency. He could not identify Jeff or Andy by name but said there were two deaf boys who lived in the trailer across the drive. He had not seen them leave, but he doubted they would be up so early because they "had one hell of a party last night: beer, food, girls, and the whole nine yards." He continued, "There must have been twenty deaf people over there. You would think deaf folks wouldn't make much noise because they talk with their hands, but they must sign some real funny jokes because I never heard so much laughing in my life. I think it was somebody's birthday because one of the girls brought a cake with candles."

Jo proceeded across the road to try to contact Jeff. The trailer was not on a solid foundation, and Jo thought she might be able to create sufficient vibration to attract their attention by shaking the door—as long as they were not sleeping too soundly. Retrieving a pair of work gloves from the trunk of the Toyota and putting them on to protect her hands, Jo approached the trailer. Grasping the doorknob with her right hand and a metal air conditioner support with her left, she planted her feet solidly on the ground and engaged her five-foot-two, 120-pound frame in violently shaking the mobile home of Jeff Kelley and Andy Sprague. An uninformed observer might have thought she was trying to dislodge the air conditioner or perhaps rock the trailer off of its blocks, because each thrust of her energy was punctuated by the swishing of her honey-blonde hair from side to side and the up-and-down motion of the window air conditioner.

When Jo ceased her exertion for a moment, either to regain her strength or to listen for any sign of movement inside, she heard a car door slam behind her and a girl's voice yell something that she could not understand. As Jo turned, she saw a rather attractive red-haired girl advancing toward her with a very angry expression on her face. The girl's words were incomprehensible, but they were accompanied by obscene hand signs that immediately told Jo that her confrontor was deaf. Concluding that the menacing young woman had mistaken her for an enemy, Jo began to back toward her car while pointing to herself and signing "DORS."

By now, a second girl had gotten out of the car and was pacing Jo in her slow, backward retreat to the Toyota. She could understand this girl, who had speech similar to the angry one. "She says she will beat your ass if you go through that door again. She heard some girl was sneaking out here to sleep with her boyfriend, Andy, and now she caught you trying to get him to open the door for you in broad daylight."

Jo felt the car against her back and quickly entered the vehicle, closing the door behind her. Snatching her wallet from her purse, she flipped it opened to display her photo ID card. Recognizing the department name, the young woman with the understandable speech shouted and signed to her friend: "DORS! DORS! It's Jeff's rehab counselor." Pointing at Jo, she continued, "We met her at the Center for Independent Living. Don't you remember?"

After further explanation and reassurance, Andy's girlfriend apologized and offered to help raise the sleeping occupants of the trailer. By then, Jo did not feel up to an hour-long counseling session that she would have to conduct in sign language. Therefore, she left a note in the mailbox informing Jeff that she would return the following Friday at 3:00 P.M. Jo turned the car's air conditioner to high and settled back to relax and restore her serenity during the hour drive to her next client in the quiet village of Shawneetown on the tranquil bank of the Ohio River.

PART THREE

LEARNING TO TRAVEL WITH BLINDNESS: ORIENTATION AND MOBILITY INSTRUCTION

[T]he greatest need of those who cannot see is, and always will be, communication on all levels of existence with those who can see.
　—Alan Eaton, *Beauty for the Sighted and the Blind*

D r. Eaton's words are as relevant today as when they were written more than a quarter century ago. In this information age, almost every human activity, from ordering a Big Mac to performing one's job, depends on the ability to process written communication, much of which is in the form of icons and other graphic symbols not readily accessible to blind persons. If, however, the most severe problem of those who are blind continues to be the speedy and accurate processing of written communication, the second most serious problem remains the difficulty of traveling from one point to another in order to engage in social and economic activity.

In fact, the problem of mobility outdates the problem of written communication by hundreds of years. Reports of blind people using canes to explore their paths date back at least as far as the

Middle Ages, when bands of roving blind folk traveled about Europe seeking food and shelter, using their long canes to find their way and sometimes to attack unwilling benefactors. Independent travel, requiring extreme concentration of one's perceptual and physical abilities, has remained a serious challenge for persons who cannot see down to the present day, indicated by the overwhelming number of blind persons who employ the cane method for independent mobility. One of the stories included in this chapter, "Hold Old Sam," focuses on the teaching of cane travel by rehabilitation teachers, who assumed responsibility for this phase of adjustment to blindness between the introduction of the long cane method by Dr. Richard Hoover and the general availability of college-trained instructors of mobility to agencies serving the civilian blind. "The Mobility Race," on the other hand, describes the work of a college-trained instructor and explores some of the issues created by the birth of this new discipline.

HOLD OLD SAM

I stepped out of the elevator on the fourth floor of the Chancellor Hotel in Champaign, Illinois, used the back of my right hand to count four doors, and entered with the magnetic room key that the desk clerk had marked with a piece of tape so I could insert it properly without sight. When the large box of Braille books slid from my shoulder and thudded to the floor, John Craig, my roommate for the training conference on the 1992 Rehabilitation Amendments, asked, "What's in the box, the Bible?"

"*Playboy*, complete with Braille pictures," I quipped, although we both knew that the hundreds of pages contained the sections of the Illinois Administrative Rules incorporating the 1992 Federal Rehabilitation Amendments. After a few minutes of small talk, I headed for the bar, also located on the fourth floor, where free drinks and popcorn were served to hotel guests between 5:00 and 6:00 P.M.

At least half of the administrative and supervisory employees of the Illinois Department of Rehabilitation Services were already in the bar partaking of the largess. Picking up two free beers from the bar, I inched over to the table where I heard the voices of Rick Regan, a regional administrator of the Bureau of Blind Services, and his rehabilitation teacher supervisor, Verle

Wessel. After we debated the merits of professional education versus apprentice training for rehabilitation teachers of the blind, Verle offered to share an amusing story resulting from his work.

This particular situation occurred when Verle was a young rehabilitation teacher of the blind. He had entered this profession in part because of his graduate training in counseling and in part because of success in coping with his own blindness. Verle said he had been teaching independent living skills to newly blinded persons for only about one year when he first visited Sam Adkins in the living room of the comfortable home he shared with his wife, Tilley, on a quiet street in Champaign. Having learned of the beneficial effect on the rehabilitation process of engaging newly blinded people in constructive activities as early as possible, Verle focused his attention on identifying tasks that would interest Sam and build his self-confidence. During this initial home interview, Verle guided the conversation, searching for those pastimes and hobbies that had been particularly rewarding for Sam, with the purpose of encouraging him to resume those that did not require vision. The problem was that almost everything Sam enjoyed required excellent vision. As a young man, he had been an amateur jockey, switching to race car driving in middle life. He had earned his living as a truck driver, and his primary reading interests were newspapers and racing forms. In short, there wasn't much that Verle had to teach that Sam felt would help him. As Sam put it, "There ain't much a sixty-year-old blind guy can do that's worth doin'."

Mrs. Adkins, who was preparing dinner, interjected the comment from the kitchen that she had plenty to keep Sam busy. Sam's response was, "Who the hell wants to be busy, anyhow?" He told Verle firmly that he had no interest in learning to make home repairs and that cooking was his wife's job. The only suggestion that sparked a little interest was Verle's offer to teach cane travel. Sam said he had enjoyed walking when he went squirrel hunting, so he told Verle to bring a cane on his next visit to begin teaching him to use it.

During the next six weeks, Sam learned that the white cane could be much more than an inanimate object once a person was taught to use it effectively and interpret the information conveyed through touch and hearing. By swinging the cane about one inch above the terrain and tapping it at the point where he would take his next step, Sam found he could locate even low obstacles and depressions in his path. The sound of the cane told him whether his next step would be on grass, concrete, or some other surface. He learned to follow the right edge of the sidewalk by extending his cane swing a little to the right and detecting grass, retaining walls, or some other "shore-line." Finally, he learned to walk straight across streets by aligning the toes of his shoes with the curb, imagining he could see the sidewalk directly across the street and heading briskly for it.

By the fourth mobility lesson, Sam's enthusiasm for learning to walk about his neighborhood was definitely on the increase. He was eager to begin the assignment that Verle outlined for him as soon as he had correctly descended his front steps. Verle's directions were for Sam to combine his knowledge of the neighborhood with what he had learned about using the cane, employing sound and touch to determine bearings and directions, and making mental maps of his travel route. Sam was then instructed to select a business or some other destination a few blocks from his home and apply his knowledge of traveling without sight to plan a route and then take Verle to the established destination. Sam seemed to be in deep thought for at least two minutes while Verle waited patiently, noting the tap of a woodpecker in a nearby tree, the odor of fresh asphalt from a neighbor's newly oiled driveway, the high-pitched whine of an electric drill several houses down the street, and the heavy traffic on Highway 45, located two blocks east of Sam's property. Verle did not want Sam to choose a destination involving the crossing of this busy highway, because his training had not included techniques for traveling in heavy traffic. He was relieved when, after drawing an imaginary map of the walk with his cane, Sam chose a route to the west of his home where traffic would be light. "Let's see if this old dog can relearn a couple of old tricks," Sam said with a chuckle, starting off down the street away from the heavy traffic on Route 45.

"Where are we going?" asked Verle as he hurried to keep up with Sam, who was making excellent use of his newly learned mobility skills to cross the first street and begin walking north at a brisk pace.

"Don't worry! You'll find out when we get there," Sam answered. Sam walked two blocks north and one block further west, becoming lost only once when he had to cross a gas station drive and veered in toward the pumps. He recovered his bearings quickly by using the sound of the passing cars to guide him back to the sidewalk. Just past the gas station, Verle heard a large fan and smelled the odor of frying fish from what he thought was a tavern, due to the slight odor of beer mixed with the fish smell. Verle wondered if this was Sam's chosen destination.

Sure enough, Sam climbed the two steps and entered through the screen door as though he had miraculously regained his sight. By the time Verle was able to negotiate the steps with his cane, find the doorknob, and get inside, Sam was being greeted by several people at the bar, and a gruff male voice, probably the bartender, Verle thought, was telling someone to vacate the corner stool. "That was always Sam's stool," the gruff voice said, "and we've been savin' it for him even though he ain't been here to sit on it since he went blind." Everyone stopped talking, and the gruff voice from behind the bar continued in a subdued manner, "Gosh, Sam, I didn't mean to insult you by mentioning your blindness. I'm sorry!"

"Don't worry about insulting me," Sam laughed as he reclaimed his corner stool. "I'm so happy to be back with my old friends and hear your gravelly voice again, Jess, that nothing could insult me. Besides, coming down here gives me a chance to get away from the Old Lady for a while." Sam's disclaimer of hurt feelings seemed to relieve the tension, and everybody resumed talking at once.

A female voice, which Verle later discovered belonged to Mickey, the bartender's wife, said, as she planted a loud kiss on Sam, "I'll bet the Old Lady is glad to get rid of you, you old fart." Sam gave Mickey a big hug and introduced Verle to her and all the others as the teacher responsible for "getting me out of my rockin' chair and back among the living."

Sam and Verle passed a pleasant half hour in Jess's Tavern. Sam caught up on what had been going on in the lives of the other patrons and filled them in on his activities, or lack thereof, since acute glaucoma had totally blinded him in a matter of hours. When someone asked if the glaucoma had been painful, Sam replied that it was the worst pain he had ever experienced, with the exception being the mental torture of instant blindness without any prior preparation for this condition. He again credited Verle with "helping me rejoin the living," explaining that he considered the day Verle placed the white cane in his hand as "the first day of my new life." At this point in the reunion of Sam and his friends, Jess said he was so happy to see Sam out and about again that he was providing a round of drinks on the house.

In a few minutes, Sam told his friends that he was in the middle of a travel training lesson and that Verle had only so much time to teach him before moving on to the next blind student. Again shaking hands with his friends, he said he would be seeing them often, now that he could navigate to Jess and Mickey's place. With this pronouncement, Sam stepped through the front door and led the way back to his house without a hitch.

Verle left on a two-week vacation, leaving Sam the assignment of traversing routes to the neighborhood grocery store and dry cleaner, neither of which was more than three blocks from Sam's home nor involved the crossing of busy streets. Being the well-organized and conscientious teacher that he still is, Verle was surprised and a little concerned when he was greeted upon his return by his secretary, Bonnie Porter, with the message that he was to report to his supervisor, Bruce McKenzie, at once. To Verle's question regarding why Bruce wanted to talk with him, Bonnie could only say that a lady had been waiting for Bruce when he arrived. As Bruce escorted her into his office, the lady was saying something about the poor teaching service her husband had received from this agency.

While storing his lunch and hanging his coat, Verle mentally reviewed the assignments he had given his students for any-thing that could have been too difficult or unsafe. Had he left Braille writing equipment without thoroughly teaching its use, given a cooking assignment without teaching the basic kitchen safety techniques, or, perhaps, made a cane travel as-signment that was too advanced and there had been an acci-dent? That was it: Sam Adkins had been hurt, and Mrs. Adkins was blaming him. Verle knew Bruce McKenzie as a supervisor who adhered to high standards of rehabilitation teaching and who expected his staff to do the same. Bruce had a national reputation in the profession, having served as president of the Mid-America Conference of Rehabilitation Teachers and as a leader in establishing standards for teachers that were adopted by the National Accreditation Counsel of Agencies for the Blind. Verle was also aware that Bruce was currently defending the competency of blind teachers in a national controversy regard-ing mobility training. Because of his position in this debate, Bruce might not appreciate one of his teachers overestimating the competency of a student involved in an accident, even if the teacher was not at fault. Verle collected his thoughts and his courage and opened the door to Bruce's office.

McKenzie's rich Kentucky drawl greeted Verle. "Come on in, Hoss. Mrs. Adkins, here, would like to have a word with you about her husband." Verle greeted the lady seated across from Bruce and asked her to explain her concern.

"I just think it's not right to come into my home and influ-ence my husband to start going all over the place when he's totally blind." To Verle's inquiry whether Sam had been injured during his walks, Mrs. Adkins replied, "Certainly not. I'll bet he could find his way to Gibson City with that cane and not get a scratch."

This last statement baffled Verle. If Sam was as safe a trav-eler as Mrs. Adkins thought, why was she so angry at the teacher who had taught him safe cane travel? Verle's expression must have revealed his bewilderment, for she resumed her answer to his question about Sam having an accident. "My complaint is not that you didn't teach him to get about safely. If anything, you taught Sam too well. I had been trying for at least twenty years to keep Sam out of that tavern, and, God forgive me, when he went blind, I finally succeeded. This staying at home was the only good thing about Sam's going blind. Most of the time, he was sad and wouldn't try to do anything for himself, but at least he didn't stop at Jess's Tavern on his way home from work every afternoon."

Bruce said Mrs. Adkins's problem was a little like that of a farmer he knew back in Kentucky. This fellow had the best coon dog in the county. Old Blue, as the dog was called, never let a coon get away once the farmer had climbed the tree where the coon was hiding and shook him out. Well, one night, the farmer left his son holding Old Blue by the collar as he carefully climbed to the limb next to where the coon was perched. Just as he reached to shake the adjacent limb, the farmer's limb broke, and the last thing he remembered before striking the hard earth was his own voice yelling, "Hold Old Blue!" Bruce said it seemed to him that what Mrs. Adkins needed was a way to "hold Old Sam," or at least slow him down a little.

"You put things in colorful words, like my grandfather who came here from Virginia, but you're right. I could stand Sam going down there two or three times a week if he just wouldn't stay so long."

Bruce politely asked Mrs. Adkins if she had any reluctance about entering a tavern and how Sam would feel about her doing so. She replied that she had been in such a place only once or twice in her life because Sam thought it was not proper conduct for a wife and mother to spend time in bars.

"Well, there's how we can slow Old Sam down, or at least get him home in time for dinner." He then suggested that Tilley Adkins, mother of four and grandmother of seven, inform Sam that, on those days when he visited his friends at Jess's Tavern, she would meet him there for a drink about five o'clock—or whatever time she wanted him home. She liked the idea and said she would try it.

Every so often during the time Verle continued teaching Sam Braille and other subjects he decided to study, Mrs. Adkins would report on the success of her strategy for getting Sam home on time, and she had to meet him for a drink only once shortly after her visit to Verle's office.

1 2

THE MOBILITY RACE

W iping the perspiration from his spectacles and replacing them on his face, Oscar Severe opened the
last of the five case files placed on the desk before
him some two hours before by Daniel Foster, his field work
supervisor, and remarked, "Nancy Lucas—an interesting name.
I wonder if it's Greek?"

"I wouldn't know," replied Dan Foster, a Bostonian who had
completed the graduate program in parapetology at Boston
College only two years before and was already supervising
graduate interns in his capacity of orientation specialist at the Industrial Home for the Blind in Chicago. "Besides," he continued, "the etymology of students' names has no relevance to
the teaching of parapetology, as taught in Baston," which was
the way Dan pronounced Boston. Oscar, who was from Tennessee and was in his last semester in the orientation and mobility program at Western Michigan University, thought Dan had
a strange way of pronouncing certain words, but he seemed to
be very competent in teaching blind people to travel by using
the long cane method developed by Dr. Richard Hoover for
training blinded veterans of World War II, and that was what
really counted with the interns, anyway. It seemed to Oscar that
Dan was a little overzealous in maintaining his professional im-

age, which sometimes caused him to seem condescending and humorless. He got the impression that Dan considered parapetologists, the name bestowed on those teachers of cane travel who graduated from Boston College, superior to orientation and mobility teachers, the name bestowed on Western Michigan graduates.

Dan's voice interrupted Oscar's thoughts. "Why not take your glasses off? Perspiration is collecting on your lenses, and you could, no doubt, read better without them, considering the excellent lighting in this office." It was true; the first floor of the three-story residence building, constructed in 1895, had been converted into office space in the 1950s and retrofitted with very bright fluorescent lights, but the modernization of the facility had not included air conditioning. Oscar hesitated to admit any weakness because he sensed that, somehow, it might lower Dan's professional confidence in him. If he removed his eyeglasses, he knew he would have to place his nose almost against the case file before he could read it, so he could see no way to conceal his extremely poor vision.

"You see, Dan, I'm legally blind without my glasses," Oscar admitted. "I began wearing them in fourth grade when my books were reduced to standard size print. My glasses kept me from competing in contact sports in high school and college, which is why I took up such activities as hiking, bowling, and skeet shooting." He hoped that mentioning skeet shooting, which requires rapid visual monitoring and accurate eye-hand coordination, would allay any concern Dan might have about his visual capacity to assure the safety of blind mobility students, but Dan's next comment informed Oscar that his vision was still a factor in Dan's professional assessment of him.

"Were there any stipulations on your mobility practice by the WMU Graduate School, such as a requirement that you wear corrective lenses when teaching parapetology?"

"The subject never came up," Oscar answered. "I had an unrestricted driver's license and never had any problem keeping track of my students, even without my glasses, so I guess the WMU professors were satisfied."

Dan emitted a disparaging grunt, which Oscar interpreted to mean, "Such lack of attention to visual requirements would not be tolerated in a first-class school like Boston College."

Oscar ventured the opinion that he had difficulty understanding the need for the requirement that mobility instructors possess visual acuity of 20-20. "In most states, 20-50 qualifies a person for a driver's license, and it would seem that anyone who can drive a car in traffic would have adequate vision to supervise a blind mobility student, even in heavy traffic."

"Basically, I agree with you, Oscar. Furthermore, I'll let you in on a little-known reason for that requirement." Dan lighted his Dutchmaster cigar and continued. "After World War II, the more responsible leaders in blind rehabilitation observed the efficient way in which veterans used the long cane method developed by Dr. Hoover and realized that this method could enable blind people to move independently within the mainstream. The primary problem in making this system available to all blind persons would be resistance from the large numbers of blind teachers, in our field, who would refuse to adopt this new system for themselves or teach it because of their devotion to their own individual travel techniques developed over a lifetime. Rather than spend years trying to gain acceptance for the Hoover method, it was decided that the profession of parapetology would be created with all new practitioners who would accept this clearly superior method without prejudice."

"Are you saying that the reason for requiring mobility instructors to have normal vision was to bar blind teachers from our profession?" Oscar interrogated.

Dan leaned far back in his swivel chair and slowly exhaled a cloud of cigar smoke, which blotted out the fluorescent light for a few seconds. "That's substantially what happened. Of course, safety of students was a major factor in incorporating a vision requirement into the professional qualifications, but the need to rid the Hoover method of efforts to weaken its effectiveness by including practitioners who would incorporate their own unscientific travel techniques was a primary, unwritten rationale for rigid adherence to the 20-20 vision requirement."

Dan suggested that they should turn their attention to Oscar's last student file if they wanted to finish staffing before the dinner chimes sounded. Glancing at the social and educational history, Oscar noted that his student, Nancy Lucas, had graduated from the state school for the blind the previous May at the head of her class, was the youngest child of Alice and Phillip Lucas who operated a dairy farm in central Illinois, and had been totally blind since birth from retrolental fibroplasia, a thickening of the retina created by the administration of excess oxygen to premature infants. Her I.Q. was 121, and her teachers reported that she traveled about the campus without difficulty, demonstrated excellent orientation when participating in swimming and other sports, and was chosen for leading roles in school plays.

When Oscar encountered Nancy in the student lounge after dinner, he knew why she was chosen for dramatic leads. With her soft blonde hair, angelic face with deep blue eyes, perfectly proportioned figure, and a voice like Marilyn Monroe's, it would have taken a miracle for the drama teacher to find a competitor for Nancy. Oscar watched her move about the lounge with ease, seeming to sense when she risked bumping into an object or invading another person's body space. He was sure Nancy's drama teacher had worked hard with her on such elements of stage presence as posture, how to manage her hands so she did not appear to be groping in the air like some of the other young blind people in the lounge, and projecting an alert, self-assured body image. It seemed to Oscar that Miss Nancy Lucas would be an ideal mobility student.

When he approached her the next morning after breakfast and informed her that he would be her mobility instructor, Nancy was enthusiastic about learning her way around Chicago but hastened to explain that she had received very little cane training in the past. She had simply begun learning to get about her immediate residence as a small child and kept widening her travel area as she grew older. By the time she went to the school for the blind, she had developed travel techniques, such as walking in a straight line, making ninety-degree turns and remembering them so she could retrace her route, and using sounds, odors, and landmarks, such as the iron grating in the walk at the turn into the dining hall, to navigate her environment. However, she expressed some doubt as to her capacity to learn how to travel independently in a large city, which would necessitate planning and negotiating complicated routes in unknown areas. Nancy said that she had been accustomed to adding an occasional route to a thoroughly familiar area such as her home or the school, but she was not sure she could master a totally new environment like Chicago. Oscar assured her that, with modern mobility techniques, she would be able to apply her present techniques effectively to any new situation.

"This city is just a cluster of small towns made up of basic geometric shapes such as rectangles and triangles," Oscar explained.

"Geometry was never my best subject," Nancy said with a laugh. She explained that she could understand the various patterns when they were presented in raised lines in her Braille text, but she could never succeed in expanding these shapes to large areas discussed by her teachers and family, such as acres, buildings, and square miles.

Oscar assured Nancy that she would have no difficulty in learning to travel in Chicago and scheduled a lesson for 9:00 the next day when she would begin mastering the Hoover cane method. He then conducted diagnostic teaching interviews with his five other clients and scheduled lessons for each. These people, two women and three men, had become blind later in life. Four retained sufficient sight to recognize objects, and all could construct a visual map of a travel route consisting of streets, buildings, open areas, and other environmental features from pre-blind memory. None had ever used a white cane before, and all five expressed a feeling of embarrassment at the thought of using one in public, although none said this embarrassment at appearing blind to others would keep them from using the long cane—at least until they went back home to their friends and families. Oscar was confident that his counseling and the success each would experience in traveling around the city with the long cane would dissipate this embarrassment.

After spending a couple of hours exploring foot travel routes in the neighborhood of the Industrial Home in order to familiarize himself with the sounds, odors, and other nonvisual clues his students would be using to guide themselves around the area, Oscar turned in early and dreamed of being totally blind while feeling his way through a desolate area filled with large boulders, cliffs, quicksand, and other dangerous obstacles with only the voice of Nancy Lucas somewhere ahead to guide him.

He was relieved to hear the wake-up chimes and confirm that he was not blind. He dressed quickly, breakfasted on coffee and cereal, and waited on the bench next to the Marshall Boulevard entrance for Nancy to appear for her first mobility lesson. She was dressed in an attractive pink blouse and matching knee-length skirt, with a straw hat perched on her hair to shade her face from the September sun, which still had enough summer heat to redden fair skin.

"I'm anxious to begin learning about this man, Hoover, who has a method that will teach me to get around Chicago," she announced. "By the way, is he related to former President Hoover?"

Oscar explained that Richard Hoover was an eye doctor who had become interested in the mobility problems of blind people when he worked at the Maryland School for the Blind while in medical school. Oscar then proceeded to guide her in the performance of the basic long cane technique, which consisted of gripping the shaft in the thumb and three fingers with the index finger pointing down the shaft toward the walk. With a wrist movement, the cane is tapped lightly near the spot where each step will bring the traveler's foot in order to detect objects, steps, and the like on the walkway. Every few steps, the cane arc can be extended slightly to the right to locate the edge of the walkway. By combining this cane technique with her previously acquired strategies for following travel routes, Nancy was able to navigate herself around the entire block on which the Industrial Home for the Blind was located during this first one-hour travel lesson.

During the succeeding weeks in September, Nancy had mobility lessons Monday through Friday, consistently augmenting her basic cane technique with strategies for ascending and descending steps, crossing streets by listening to the flow of traffic, locating and boarding buses by listening for the sound of the automatic door opening, locating business establishments by the sounds and odors emanating from their opened doors, and many others that could make her independent travel around Chicago a reality. By the beginning of October, Oscar was switching the emphasis of Nancy's lessons to the independent planning and traversing of new travel routes involving walking with the long cane and using the elevated train, bus, and streetcar systems. She had no difficulty mastering the use of these systems but was unable to plan and execute new travel routes to unknown destinations involving such concepts as the empty space between buildings and other objects in her travel environment, the spatial relationship between herself and other pedestrians walking in different directions, and how streets and railways divided the city into geometric shapes that were parts of larger geometric patterns, such as neighborhoods and the entire city; neither could she maintain a mental map of what was across the street from her. Oscar tried to convey these concepts by preparing raised-line maps for Nancy to study and found that she could plot and trace a route with her fingers on an eleven-inch-square raised line map, but she seemed incapable of applying this knowledge to the actual movement of her body through the city to reach a location to which she had not previously traveled.

One rainy morning in late October, after several unsuccessful attempts to describe the relationship of the various streets surrounded by the rectangle of elevated railway tracks known as the Chicago Loop, Nancy vented her frustration by pounding her small fist on Oscar's desk and shouting, "That Dr. Hoover may be a whiz-bang at teaching blind soldiers to tap their canes, but he doesn't know a hoot about teaching the ones who have been blind all their lives, like me!"

Seeing the tears welling up in her eyes, Oscar leaned across the desk to place a tissue in Nancy's hand and pat her comfortingly on the arm. "Listen, Nancy, you're one of the best cane travelers I know. You've hit a little rough going at this particular stage of your training, but, believe me, you will be plotting out trips all over this city by the time you're ready to leave here for secretarial college." Oscar hoped he was not being too optimistic. He certainly wanted to be encouraging to Nancy, but something about her realistic and honest manner of encountering the world informed him that she could lose confidence in a teacher who misled her in order to spare her feelings.

Patting her eyes with the tissue, Nancy remarked, with a touch of anger tinged with a note of accusation, "Oscar, you would be an attractive man if you hadn't started imitating Mr. Foster by smoking those smelly cigars."

Instead of assuring her that he would not smoke in her presence, Oscar immediately decided to continue smoking during lessons, because this might tend to dampen any romantic ideas Nancy might develop about him. She was an extremely comely young woman, and the more professional their relationship remained, the less chance there would be for relationship complications. Her comment that he could be attractive if he gave up cigars caused Oscar to wonder if a part of her anger could be a subconscious cover for a schoolgirl infatuation. He had learned in counseling courses about the process of transference in which women in crisis attribute characteristics of husbands and other loved ones to their doctors and teachers. Oscar also knew himself well enough to realize that this process could go in the other direction, and the last thing he needed was word of a romantic entanglement with a student brought to Dan Foster, that pillar of academic propriety.

Intending to bolster Nancy's confidence in her potential for becoming a thoroughly independent cane traveler, Oscar shifted the conversation to Nancy's forthcoming solo trip from the Chicago Loop to the Industrial Home for the Blind. He explained that she would be required to locate public transportation from a drop-off point somewhere in the Loop and return to the Home without assistance. Nancy admitted reservations regarding her readiness to plan a new route from the Loop back to the rehabilitation center, although she was sure she could find her way back if she were taught the route ahead of time. Oscar again expressed confidence in her ability to learn advanced mobility and said that he would discuss her case with his supervisor, who would be able to suggest techniques that would enable Nancy to travel in unknown areas.

With his other students progressing satisfactorily, Oscar continued to ponder the paradox presented by Nancy Lucas. On the one hand, her sensory alertness, compass directions and bearings, techniques for crossing streets in heavy traffic, and use of public transit were superior to any of the others, but she could make effective use of these skills only after being taught a particular route. On the other hand, his other students had little or no difficulty in applying nonvisual travel methods to the independent exploration of new areas of the city. John Denowski had found his way to a Russian Orthodox Church, Marie Evans had figured out the route to visit her sister in Oak Park, and Travis James had found a nightclub in Cicero. In planning and executing trips to new places, the other students were far more advanced than Nancy. What frustrated Oscar was that these other students were steadily improving in those areas in which Nancy excelled while she seemed at a standstill in learning strategies for new exploration.

On the Friday after Nancy had angrily hit his desk, Oscar requested that he and Dan Foster devote their entire weekly supervisory conference to the case of Nancy Lucas. Being a frugal man in time as well as money, Dan readily agreed to this agenda, for he was aware that Oscar's other students were progressing well in all areas and required only a brief review. Oscar had briefly mentioned Nancy's problem with conceptualizing large geographical areas at previous conferences, and Dan had also heard some students talking at dinner about an argument between Nancy and Oscar in Oscar's office the day before.

Oscar reviewed his work with Nancy, beginning with his original assessment and ending with the last lesson when she had become angry because of her lack of progress in route planning. Dan began to focus on Oscar's method for conveying large concepts to his students. Oscar had used the same basic approach with Nancy that he had found successful with his other students, all of whom had visual memory. Dan explained that when people become blind in adult life, they retain visual memories of streets, blocks, railway systems, and most other components that make up their world. People blind from birth, on the other hand, have no visual memory and must conceptualize spatial relationships based on hearing and touch. "Whereas a seeing person can encompass a panoramic view of everything around her and retain these stored pictures to construct visual maps in real time and space whenever she receives verbal descriptions or feels raised maps, Nancy can conceptualize only as much as she can feel with both hands."

Oscar thought for a while and asked how congenitally blind persons develop understanding of large areas. "I am not sure that any sighted person really knows," Dan admitted. "All we are certain of is that some people who have never had sight develop the ability to travel independently to places they have never been before, while others never seem to acquire this skill."

"Am I going to have to tell Nancy that she will have to depend on someone to show her the way every time she wants to go to a new place?" Oscar asked with a note of panic.

"Not necessarily," Dan reassured him. "If you place heavy emphasis on transferring tactile maps and verbal information into Nancy's auditory and time memory, you may be able to start some kind of mental process that she can use for adding new travel routes to her data base. In other words, if she can learn to anticipate how long she will have to ride or walk between points, the turns she will make, and the sounds and smells she will encounter along the way, she may become an independent traveler."

Oscar thought for a while and then speculated: "If I understand what you are saying, it seems that Nancy's primary thought structure must be based on touch sequences instead of large visual pictures. Therefore, if I can get her to mentally project these touch sequences into the future and think of the time it would take her to travel this projected route, she might be able to move about unfamiliar areas without prior instruction."

"Something like that," Dan said slowly, "but you're really in uncharted waters when trying to teach people who have never seen to conceptualize such visual phenomena as depth, contrast, movement through space, and relative size of distant objects."

Dan and Oscar had analyzed Nancy's learning style about as thoroughly as their own vision-dominated learning methods would permit. As Oscar was leaving, Dan placed a restraining hand lightly on his arm. "Remember! Plan and conduct your lessons in such a manner that the student does not lose face if you find she is absolutely unable to master unknown areas."

Oscar restructured his teaching style with Nancy, emphasizing connections between sounds and her location and distance from objects much more than explaining how the world looks to seeing people. He tried such techniques as having Nancy listen to her voice echoing off a building across a quiet street as a way of reinforcing the fact that the building, which she could not see, was actually there. Nancy seemed to be gaining confidence from such unusual learning experiences and even took a short trip to a beauty salon located in an unfamiliar neighborhood.

One morning in early November, Nancy was practicing ascending and descending stairs in the elevated train station at California and Marshal Boulevard when Oscar announced that he had scheduled her solo trip from the Loop for the following Friday afternoon. "You would have to schedule me for Friday when the Loop is crawling with people for me to bump into and lose my direction."

"Come on, Nancy," Oscar chided, "you never get lost. You're one of the most competent cane travelers I have ever known. So what's bothering you about the Loop trip?"

"You guys that can see really get my goat sometimes. You expect us to travel in downtown Chicago without any sight while you are watching every move we make with your sight. If you had to find your way around this place without eyesight, you would have a better idea of our problems."

Oscar controlled his anger and explained patiently that he had spent many hours practicing cane travel while wearing a blindfold.

"How many times have you traveled around the Loop wearing one?" Nancy taunted. Oscar knew he should not let a snip of a girl bait him into doing something stupid—like letting her travel back from the Loop totally unattended. It was agency practice to observe students making their solo trip from a distance of about a city block. Dan would certainly not approve of such irresponsibility. Nevertheless, when Nancy said, "Well, how many times?," Oscar was hooked.

"All right, young lady, we will conduct a little experiment. When I drop you off in the Loop, I will don my blindfold, and the one who arrives back at the Industrial Home first will buy lunch."

Nancy clapped her hands and said, "You're on, Mr. Mobility Teacher."

During the next week, Oscar allocated a two-hour period for a close visual analysis of the exact route he guessed Nancy would follow from her drop-off near the Fanny Mae candy store between Clark and LaSalle Streets on the north side of Randolph. He decided to warn Nancy about some of the obstacles, such as the construction excavation near the Sherman Hotel. It wouldn't do for her to sustain even a very minor injury while he was fumbling around the Loop wearing a blindfold instead of monitoring her progress. Dan would skin him alive.

The following Friday dawned clear with a crisp breeze blowing in off the lake. Oscar felt confident and invigorated by the chill punctuated with the warm sun rays filtering between the skyscrapers as he and Nancy walked down Randolph Street to the front entrance of the Sherman Hotel. From there, she had been instructed to proceed to the Fanny Mae candy store, where she was to purchase half a pound of fudge and find her way back to the Industrial Home. She was aware that she would not have visual monitoring and back-up from Oscar, since he would also be traveling blind, but she assured him that she had absolutely no concern for her safety.

Oscar watched Nancy enter the store. After waiting until no one was watching, he pulled on his blindfold, lit one of Dan's cigars, and leaned against the wall to enjoy the sun until he could be certain Nancy had left the candy store and was traveling toward the subway. When he heard her assure a pedestrian that she knew how to locate the subway, Oscar quietly moved off ahead of her. He took a circuitous route so she would not follow the sound of his cane. He walked south on Clark to Washington, east to Dearborn, and doubled back a half block to stairs leading down to the subway.

He had taught several blind people to board trains and buses by listening for the opening door sound, but he had never performed this activity without being able to see the approaching vehicle. The all-encompassing sound of the approaching train and the sensation that it was rushing directly at him almost caused Oscar to panic and rip off his blindfold; he grabbed a support column just to reassure himself that he was several feet from the edge of the platform. He decided to be more understanding of his students' feelings of panic when standing near a moving train.

When the noise of the train ceased and the sound of the automatic door came from directly in front of him, Oscar sighed with relief and stepped into the car, first checking with his cane to be sure he was not stepping between the cars. Luckily, the first seat was empty, and Oscar collapsed into it. He took a long pull on his cigar and settled down to count the stops and curves in the track until he reached the California Station. He could not always understand the names of the stops called by the conductor, so counting the stops gave an extra margin of security.

Oscar was on his feet and ready to step onto the platform as soon as the train came to a complete stop at the California Station. Exiting the train, he found the wall and moved along it until he located the stairs leading down to the street, for the train had exited the subway tunnel after going under the Chicago River and was three stories above street level at the California Station.

Traveling with more confidence in the area he had explored

wearing a blindfold, Oscar enjoyed the remainder of his cigar until he reached the bench in front of the Industrial Home. A cane touched the bench and someone sat down beside him. Oscar's first thought was that Dan had caught him wandering around wearing a blindfold while his totally blind student was searching her way through the streets of Chicago. Snatching the blindfold from his eyes, Oscar was dumbfounded to see Nancy relaxing on the bench beside him.

"Nancy, are you all right?" he almost shouted. "Did you run into trouble? Did the police drive you back?"

"Oscar! Don't you know that we blind folks can travel faster than you sighted guys wearing blindfolds?" she asked with a little laugh.

"You mean to say you came back on the train? How on God's green earth did you figure out the travel route and get here before I did?"

"Didn't have to figure it out," Nancy stated. "I only had to follow you. You thought you were pretty cute going around that block on the way to the train just to try confusing me, but I was right behind you all the way: sat across from you in the train, heard you excuse yourself when you bumped into that lady with the shopping bag, and would have been here on the bench waiting for you if my slipper hadn't come off when it caught in a grating as we left the el station at California, making me miss the traffic light."

"I still don't get it, Nancy," Oscar said, lighting another cigar. "My hearing is not as sharp as yours, but not even you could have followed the sound of my cane in that noisy subway."

"Elementary, Watson," she declared in an exaggerated English accent. "You see, my dear fellow, I had only to follow the odor of your foul-smelling cigar!"

A Blindness Rehabilitation
Glossary

This glossary is provided to facilitate the use of this text for graduate work in rehabilitation of the blind. In particular, students can use the glossary to read the stories within a professional framework by applying the terminology and concepts below. It is also provided to give the general reader a more specific understanding of some of the issues and activities central to rehabilitation of the blind.

Adaptive Labeling. A variety of techniques (including tactile marking, Braille and raised lettering, replicas affixed to containers, and large print) that enable persons with visual impairments to identify personal items, products, tools, and documents and to read gauges such as thermostats and other appliance panels.

Auditory Monitoring. The process of forming mental constructs of the environment by interpreting auditory perceptions.

Bibliotherapy. A counseling technique for enabling persons who are visually impaired to adjust to their disability by discussing biographical, autobiographical, and fictional accounts of persons who have experienced this disability.

Blindness Adjustment Counseling. The application of therapeutic counseling techniques for enabling persons who are blind and their associates to accept and utilize compensatory skills and equipment for successful participation in personal, social, and economic life.

Blindness Support Groups. Small groups of visually impaired persons (usually fewer than ten for maximum effectiveness) who meet regularly to share experience and information, listen to speakers on various aspects of visual adjustment and treatment, and derive emotional support from group interactions.

Body Protection Method. A cluster of techniques involving the use of arms, hands, cane, and posture to protect the head and trunk from injurious contacts with potentially dangerous objects, such as open doors, when walking in hazardous areas.

Braille Cell. A rectangular space divided into six parts for containing two vertical rows of three Braille dots that can be covered by the ball of the index finger.

Braille Dot Numbering. The assignment of numbers one through six to the spaces for embossing dots in the Braille cell; when reading, the dots are numbered from top to bottom with 1, 2, and 3 on the left side of the cell and 4, 5, and 6 on the right.

Braille Pegboard. A rectangular block, usually made of wood, with one or more sets of six holes in the pattern of the Braille cell into which students can insert pegs to form Braille characters.

Cell Printing. A technique for teaching the formation of print characters to Braille readers by utilizing the Braille dot numbers (having a student draw a line through dots 1, 2, 3, and 6 to form the letter *L*, for example).

Compensatory Skills. Skills for performing life activities without vision or with very limited vision.

Compensatory Skill Training. Instruction in using the residual senses of hearing, touch, smell, and taste to compensate for limited vision in the performance of life activities.

Contracted Braille. Advanced literacy Braille that employs a variety of contractions in order to conserve space and increase reading speed.

Corrugated Writing Board. A sheet of cardboard with raised lines corresponding to the lines on ruled stationery that is placed underneath a sheet of writing paper to provide a blind person with a tactual line guide for separating and proportioning handwriting.

Currency Identification. Techniques used by people with visual impairments for identifying and managing both paper currency and coins (including differential folding, using divided wallets, placing bills in denominational sequence, and identifying coins by their tactual characteristics).

Dot Conversion. The reversal of Braille dot numbers when embossing characters on a slate in which the dots appear on the underside of the slate facing away from the writer; thus, dots 1, 2, and 3 are embossed on the right side and 4, 5, and 6 on the left side of the cell.

Facial Vision. The interpretation of sound and temperature waves reflected from objects to infer the location, distance, size, and shape of these objects.

File Data Reversal. Transposing the data read from the top line of a print file card to the bottom line of a Braille card and proceeding to enter the remaining material in this reverse order so that, when the card is filed upside down and facing away from the student, the reversed material will appear in proper order and perspective to the student's reading fingers.

Gauge Blocks. Small pieces of wood or other materials pre-cut to prescribed dimensions used for making quick, repetitive measurements.

Handwriting Guide. A frame or template that is placed over writing paper to guide a visually impaired person in writing straight lines, entering information on preprinted forms (such as checks), or signing documents (signature guide).

Haptic Skills Instruction. Instruction in the use of touch for examining, identifying, monitoring, and manipulating (often employing craft projects, woodworking, or clay modeling as a vehicle for imparting these haptic skills).

Home Teacher of the Blind. The first formal group of rehabilitation practitioners were the home teachers dispatched by the

London Home Teaching Society in 1855 to teach embossed reading systems and home industry processes to adult blind persons.

Human Guide Method. A cluster of contact techniques that enable a sighted person to walk with a blind person in a safe, comfortable, inconspicuous manner.

Landmark. A reference point (such as a corner mailbox, street curb, incline, texture change, doorway, or some other environmental feature) that a visually impaired person can identify to establish progress toward an established goal or destination.

Lesson Plan. A logical plan for presenting a method or unit of instruction that is congruent with the unique learning style of an individual or group of individuals.

Low Vision Training. The methodology for instructing a person with limited vision in using this residual eyesight, usually in consort with other residual senses, to guide the performance of personal, social, economic, and other life activities.

Multisensory Monitoring. The process of forming mental constructs and inferences by synthesizing perceptions from two or more senses.

Nail Driving Gauge. A small block, usually made of wood, with a V-shaped cut that is placed with the point of the V where a nail is to be driven; this V can guide a blind carpenter in positioning and driving the nail straight.

Orientation and Mobility Instructor (Peripatologist). A teacher trained in the anatomical systems involved in walking and the compensatory skills required for environmental orientation without adequate vision who teaches visually impaired persons to travel independently and safely.

Reader Pacing. A technique for increasing reading speed in which teacher and student read alternate words, lines, or sentences aloud while the silent reader confirms the correctness of the spoken words; the teacher increases the reading speed by very small increments during the lesson in order to increase the student's reading pace imperceptibly.

Reference Point. An object, sound, odor, or some other identifiable feature of a visually impaired person's environment that can be used to establish one's position in relation to other objects, persons, or features of the environment.

Saw Guide. A scribe line or a straight line edge that can be clamped to a board to provide tactual guidance for sawing.

Sensory Alertness. The habit of mentally registering sensory stimuli and selectively interpreting those stimuli that are necessary for the performance of desired activities without sight or with very limited vision.

Sequential Instruction. The presentation of steps in a process, procedure, or task in a sequence based on the order in which these steps are usually performed.

Sound Localization. The skill of identifying the location of sounds in relation to the listener's spatial location and body position.

Tactual Monitoring. The process of forming mental constructs of the environment by interpreting tactile perceptions.

Tactual Scanning. Examination of a prescribed area through sense of touch; large areas are divided into segments small enough to be thoroughly covered by the hands or a hand extender such as a cane, ruler, or brush.

Teaching Outcome. The measurable performance results achieved by students who have learned a technique, method, or process.

Teaching Visual Imaging. Instructing a blind person to identify, locate, and draw other inferences about environmental features by mentally placing these features in accurate spatial perspective with the student's body position and location.

Two-Handed Braille Reading. A method of reading Braille in which the left index finger reads approximately one-third of each line and the right index finger finishes reading the line while the left hand retraces the current lines and locates the beginning of the next line.

Visual Imagery. The substitution of stored visual images for persons, objects, and other environmental features for the purpose of making inferences about one's current surroundings.

Vocational Rehabilitation Counselor of the Blind. A practitioner trained in the theories and methods of vocational guidance with special emphasis on the application to the work site of compensatory skills, adaptive equipment, and psychological strategies for functioning with little or no vision.

Alvin Roberts is a regional administrator in the Illinois Department of Human Services, Bureau of Blind Services, where he supervises rehabilitation teachers, counselors, and orientation and mobility instructors in the thirty-five southern Illinois counties. He was born in 1930 in Carbondale, Illinois, where he later attended Southern Illinois University and received his bachelor and master of science degrees in education. Many of his articles on rehabilitation teaching theory and technique have appeared in *Rehabilitation Teacher, Dialogue,* the *Journal of Blindness and Visual Impairment,* and *Re-View.* His previous books include a rehabilitation textbook, *Psychosocial Rehabilitation of the Blind,* as well as an anthology of southern Illinois-based short stories, *Tavern Tales.*